Advance Praise for *Contested Global Governance Space and Transnational Agrarian Movements*

"I highly recommend this manuscript for its high value in scientific and political debate for a critical understanding of global governance issues and core issues such as agroecology and biotechnology."
— Alessandra Corrado, Università della Calabria, Italy

"This is a very original book. Most analyses on financialization of food and agriculture are not linked to transnational agrarian movements, and most studies of transnational agrarian movements are not linked to financialization of food and agriculture. This book is the first attempt at combining analyses of the two. It is done from a scholar-activist perspective, making the book extra-ordinary and important."
— Saturnino M. Borras Jr., International Institute of Social Studies (ISS), Netherlands, co-author, *Scholar-Activism and Land Struggles*

Contested Global Governance Space and Transnational Agrarian Movements

ALSO IN THE CRITICAL DEVELOPMENT STUDIES SERIES

Contested Global Governance Space and Transnational Agrarian Movements

A Critical Development Perspective

MAURO CONTI

CRITICAL DEVELOPMENT STUDIES

To my mother Giuliana (of Alberta and Natalino, subproletarians from Trastevere in Rome), my father Carlo (of Leonilde and Alberto, peasants from the countryside of Fossombrone), and my sister Ilaria

Copyediting: Erin Seatter
Cover Design: John van der Woude, JVDW Designs
Printed and bound in Canada

Published in North America by Fernwood Publishing
2970 Oxford Street, Halifax, Nova Scotia, B3L 2W4
and 748 Broadway Avenue, Winnipeg, Manitoba, R3G 0X3
www.fernwoodpublishing.ca

Published in the rest of the world by Practical Action Publishing
27a Albert Street, Rugby, Warwickshire CV21 2SG, UK

Fernwood Publishing Company Limited gratefully acknowledges the financial support of the Government of Canada through the Canada Book Fund and the Canada Council for the Arts. We acknowledge the Province of Manitoba for support through the Manitoba Publishers Marketing Assistance Program and the Book Publishing Tax Credit. We acknowledge the Nova Scotia Department of Communities, Culture and Heritage for support through the Publishers Assistance Fund.

Library and Archives Canada Cataloguing in Publication

Title: Contested global governance space and transnational agrarian movements / Mauro Conti.
Names: Conti, Mauro (Consultant on family farming), author.
Series: Critical development studies ; 10.
Description: Series statement: Critical development studies ; 10 | Includes bibliographical references and index.
Identifiers: Canadiana (print) 20230460216 | Canadiana (ebook) 20230460240 | ISBN 9781773636337 (softcover) | ISBN 9781773636498 (PDF) | ISBN 9781773636481 (EPUB)
Subjects: LCSH: Agriculture—International cooperation—Societies, etc. | LCSH: Agriculture and politics. | LCSH: Agricultural laborers—Political activity. | LCSH: Transnationalism—Political aspects. | LCSH: Agriculture—Finance. | LCSH: Food sovereignty.
Classification: LCC HD1428 .C66 2023 | DDC 382/.41—dc23

Contents

Critical Development Studies Series

Three decades of uneven capitalist development and neoliberal globalization have devastated the economies, societies, livelihoods and lives of people around the world, especially those in societies of the Global South. Now more than ever, there is a need for a more critical, proactive approach to the study of global and development studies. The challenge of advancing and disseminating such an approach — to provide global and development studies with a critical edge — is on the agenda of scholars and activists from across Canada and the world and those who share the concern and interest in effecting progressive change for a better world.

This series provides a forum for the publication of small books in the interdisciplinary field of critical development studies — to generate knowledge and ideas about transformative change and alternative development. The editors of the series welcome the submission of original manuscripts that focus on issues of concern to the growing worldwide community of activist scholars in this field. Critical development studies (CDS) encompasses a broad array of issues ranging from the sustainability of the environment and livelihoods, the political economy and sociology of social inequality, alternative models of local and community-based development, the land and resource-grabbing dynamics of extractive capital, the subnational and global dynamics of political and economic power, and the forces of social change and resistance, as well as the contours of contemporary struggles against the destructive operations and ravages of capitalism and imperialism in the twenty-first century.

The books in the series are designed to be accessible to an activist readership as well as the academic community. The intent is to publish a series of small books (54,000 words, including bibliography, endnotes, index and front matter) on some of the biggest issues in the interdisciplinary field of critical development studies. To this end, activist scholars from across the world in the field of development studies and related academic disciplines are invited to submit a proposal or the draft of a book that conforms to the stated aim of the series. The editors will consider the submission of complete manuscripts within the 54,000-word limit. Potential authors are encouraged to submit a proposal that includes a rationale and short synopsis of the book, an outline of proposed chapters, one or two sample chapters, and a brief biography of the author(s).

Series Editors

HENRY VELTMEYER is a research professor at Universidad Autónoma de Zacatecas (Mexico) and professor emeritus of International Development Studies at Saint Mary's University (Canada), with a specialized interest in Latin American development. He is also co-chair of the Critical Development Studies Network and a co-editor of Fernwood's Agrarian Change and Peasant Studies series. The CDS *Handbook: Tools for Change* (Fernwood, 2011) was published in French by University of Ottawa Press as *Des outils pour le changement : Une approche critique en études du développement* and in Spanish as *Herramientas para el Cambio*, with funding from Oxfam UK by CIDES, Universidad Mayor de San Andrés, La Paz, Bolivia.

ANNETTE AURÉLIE DESMARAIS is the Canada Research Chair in Human Rights, Social Justice and Food Sovereignty at the University of Manitoba (Canada). She is the author of *La Vía Campesina: Globalization and the Power of Peasants* (Fernwood, 2007), which has been republished in French, Spanish, Korean, Italian and Portuguese, and *Frontline Farmers: How the National Farmers Union Resists Agribusiness and Creates our New Food Future* (Fernwood, 2019). She is co-editor of *Food Sovereignty: Reconnecting Food, Nature and Community* (Fernwood, 2010); *Food Sovereignty in Canada: Creating Just and Sustainable Food Systems* (Fernwood, 2011); and *Public Policies for Food Sovereignty: Social Movements and the State* (Routledge, 2017).

RAÚL DELGADO WISE is a research professor and director of the PhD program in Development Studies at the Universidad Autónoma de Zacatecas (Mexico). He holds the prestigious UNESCO Chair on Migration and Development and is executive director of the International Migration and Development Network, as well as author and editor of some twenty books and more than a hundred essays. He is a member of the Mexican Academy of Sciences and editor of the book series, Latin America and the

New World Order, for Miguel Angel Porrúa publishers and chief editor of the journal *Migración y Desarrollo*. He is also a member of the international working group, People's Global Action on Migration Development and Human Rights.

Acknowledgments

This work stems from my doctoral thesis, conducted under the joint supervision of the University of Calabria (UNICAL) and the International Institute of Social Studies (ISS).

First and foremost, I am most grateful to my PhD supervisors, Annamaria Vitale (UNICAL) and Jun Borras (ISS), for their guidance, encouragement, and support. They helped me approach the stimulating intersection between multiple theoretical frameworks and social struggles and the politics of social movements. Endless thanks to Alessandra Corrado at UNICAL, my behind-the-scenes mentor, who encouraged me in the first place to embark on this academic journey and promoted the *cotutela* with the ISS that forged an innovative axis between Calabria and The Hague. Without her support, I would not have written this dissertation.

Thank you to everybody at UNICAL and ISS, including my PhD comrades at UNICAL — Francesco Campolongo, Ivan Orrico, Yvonne Piersante, Silvia Rizzo, Gaelle Cariati, Claudia Giorleo, Tiziana Crispino, Manuela Scigliano, Giulio Iocco, and Carlotta Ebbreo — and the villagers at ISS — Anne Siebert, Yukari Sekine, Natacha Bruna, Nguyet Dang Bao, Salena Trammel, Daniela Andrade, Adwoa Yeboah Gyapong, Umut Kocagöz, Sergio Coronado, Mads Barbesgaard, Boaventura Monjane, Amod Shah, Daniela Calmon, Ísis Táboas, Tsegaye Moreda, Mamonova Natalia, Zoe Brent, and Ben McKey. A special thanks to Elyse Mills, who supported me through the different stages of this doctoral research, and to Alberto Alonso-Fradejas, whose extraordinary commitment from both an intellectual and a personal standpoint has been inspiring and served as crucial support to conclude my research.

Thank you to the UNICAL faculty, especially to those currently and formerly part of the Centro Studi Rurali research group, including Isabella Giunta, Carmelo Buscema, Silvia Sivini, Francesco Caruso, Annamaria Vitale, and Alessandra Corrado, and to the PhD director, Paolo Jedlowski, who has always been supportive of my unconventional research path. Special thanks to the UNICAL and ISS administrative teams, especially to Vincenzo Giacco and Sharmini Bisessar-Selvarajah.

This entire research journey has been possible thanks to the uncon-ditional trust that Antonio Onorati gave me shortly after my arrival at Centro Internazionale Crocevia in October 2010, when he opened the doors of the International Planning Committee for Food Sovereignty (IPC) and generously and without hierarchy shared with me his deep political understanding. A deeply thankful acknowledgment goes to my daily com-rades at Centro Internazionale Crocevia: Antonio Onorati, Stefano Mori, Stefano De Angelis, Danilo Licciardello, Calogero di Gloria, Edoardo Calza Bini, Eleonora Amelio, Yvonne Piersante, Aldo Orasi, Delphine Ortega, Maria Paola Boselli, Emanuele Lucci, Eleonora Mancinotti, Giulia Simula, Francesca Zaccarelli, Camilla Taranta, Viola Taormina, Alice Giro, Federica Sperti, and Benedetta Merlo.

I am profoundly indebted to the millions of activists who are part of the social movements struggling every day for food sovereignty. They are, directly or indirectly, an integral part of this research. First of all, thanks to Maria Noel Salgado Spinatelli and Andrea Ferrante, together with Javier Sanchez and Naseegh Jaffer, for the endless conversations that at the be-ginning of my journey helped me develop a new articulation of a global platform for food sovereignty. Special mention goes to Guy Kastler and the other coordinators of the IPC Working Group on Agricultural Biodiversity, Marciano da Silva and Antonio Gonzalez. I also thank Chandrika Sharma and Kuria Gathuru, who passed away during these long and intense years of struggles, and all the other leaders of the food sovereignty movement: Javier Sanchez, Angel Strapazzon, Rodolfo Grieco, Elizabeth Mpofu, Kannayian Subramaniam, Saul Vicente, Ibrahima Coulibaly, Martin Drago, Kirtana Chandrasekaran, Naseegh Jaffer, Carmen Mannarino, Sofia Monsalve, Jenny Franco, Philip Seufert, Lyda Fernanda, Sylvia Key, Carsten Pedersen, Mateus Santos, Alberto Broch, Anaru Fraser, Davinder Lamba, Nora McKeon, Flavio Valente, George Dixon, Fernando Lopez, Maede Salimi, Herman Kumara, Sherry Pictou, Natalia Laino, Ivan Mammana, Margret Muller Margaret Nakato, Editrudit Lukanga, Lalji Satia, Pat Mooney, Neth Dano, Patrick Mulvany, and among many others.

Most of the processes that are at the centre of this dissertation have been possible thanks to the professional interpreters who have volunteered over time: Audrey, Rodrigo, Joe, Stephanie, Lucia, Lara, Tono, Gaia, Ken, Gwen, Catherine, Martine, Katie, Abel, David, Monica, and more.

I conducted most of my field work within the Food and Agriculture Organization headquarters, either during official negotiations or in the corridors and the smoking rooms, where political analysis and strategies were shared. In these spaces, I had the fortune to meet incredible people who are making real the mandate of the United Nations. These people include Guilherme Brady, Francesco "Ciccio" Pierri, Anna Korzenszky, Edoardo Calza Bini, Nicole Franz, Emma McGhie, Mario Marino, and many others.

I would like to thank my amazing family for their never-ending support: my auntie Giovanna, my cousins Sandro, Mirna, Roberto, Paolo, and Priscilla, and my late grandfather Natalino, who supported me during the first four months of this doctoral research, before leaving us on February 28, 2016. Finally, and very specially, I am deeply grateful to my parents, Giuliana and Carlo, and my sister, Ilaria — who also helped with copyediting this work — for their unconditional love and support, and their example of everyday resistance to an exploitative system.

Acronyms

Copa-Cogeca	Committee of Professional Agricultural Organisations–General Confederation of Agricultural Cooperatives in the European Union
CSO	civil society organizations
DNA	deoxyribonucleic acid
DSI	digital sequence information
FAO	Food and Agriculture Organization
GATT	General Agreement on Tariffs and Trade
GMO	genetically modified organism
IFAP	International Federation of Agricultural Producers
IFOAM	International Federation of Organic Agriculture Movements
IMF	International Monetary Fund
IPC	International Planning Committee for Food Sovereignty
ITPGRFA	International Treaty on Plant Genetic Resources for Food and Agriculture
NBT	new breeding technique
NGO	nongovernmental organization
OECD	Organisation for Economic Co-operation and Development
PGRFA	plant genetic resources for food and agriculture
TAM	transnational agrarian movement
TRIPS	Trade-Related Aspects of Intellectual Property Rights
TNC	transnational corporation
WFO	World Farmers' Organisation
WTO	World Trade Organization

Introduction: A Strategic Vision for the Agrarian Institutional Guerrilla

The dilemmas of the antisystemic movements seem to be even more profound than those of the dominant forces of the world-system. In any case, without a strategy, there is no good reason to believe there is an invisible hand that will guarantee transformation in a good direction, even when and if the capitalist world-economy falls apart. (Arrighi, Hopkins, and Wallerstein 1992: 242)

For almost a decade I served as general coordinator of the secretariat of the International Planning Committee for Food Sovereignty (IPC). Convening eleven global and six subregional transnational agrarian movements (TAMs), the IPC includes more than 6,000 national member organizations and represents the voices of more than 300 million small-scale food producers. TAMs are organizations, networks, coalitions and solidarity linkages of farmers, peasants, pastoralists, and their allies that cross national boundaries and seek to influence national and global policies (Edelman and Borras 2016). Since 2003 the IPC has had a formal relationship with the United Nations Food and Agriculture Organization (FAO) to facilitate the participation of TAMs in FAO processes according to common priorities and axes of work. This includes civil society consultations leading to the FAO regional conferences, which are meant to set FAO priorities.

During my time at the IPC, I supported hundreds of delegates from TAMs in the policy dialogue spaces of the FAO. Although these delegates attended a wide range of negotiations, covering issues such as access to land to responsible investments in agriculture to recognition of small-scale fisheries, the overarching target was the same: opposing neoliberal policies in agriculture. The narrower focus of negotiations did not allow delegates to directly affect the neoliberal policy framework, but the unspoken underlying assumption was a strong connection between agricultural policies and the international economic framework.

The global movement for food sovereignty and the creation of the IPC as a space of coordination between different TAMs originated with the 1996 FAO World Food Summit and the parallel NGO Forum, held to oppose the newly established World Trade Organization (WTO). The political strategy of the time was based on using the FAO as an entry point to oppose neoliberal policies, but this did not always guide TAMs' participation in the various FAO negotiations. Indeed, in many internal meetings, IPC representatives expressed concern that their strategy was reactive and passive with respect to the priorities dictated by the FAO agenda, as participation and negotiation lines were not defined in the 1996 strategy or later updates. From this experience emerged the need to understand how agricultural policies are shaped by and reshape the economic cycle, and in particular how normative and policy dialogue in the global governance space is connected with the dominance of neoliberal policies.

The importance of prioritizing the connection with the economic cycle (e.g., oil prices, financial markets) was made clear by the world food price crisis in 2007–08, which fuelled the Arab Spring and other social uprisings in about thirty-three countries (Perez 2013; Zurayk 2011). Price fluctuations threatened global food security and increased the number of undernourished people to over 170 million (FAO 2010). This price shock showed that the global governance of agriculture is not working and is deeply affected by external economic factors, including financial ones.

Despite many analyses rooting the financialization of agriculture in post–Bretton Woods neoliberal globalization (Epstein 2005, 2008; Kotz 2008, 2015; Krippner, Lemoine, and Ravelli 2017; Palley 2007), most of them do not examine the root causes of financialization at the global level in order to then see how these play into the financialization of agriculture. One of the major limitations of these analyses, including the one presented by civil society organizations (CSOs) (CSM 2011), is that the relationship between the economic cycle and the agricultural sector remains unclear, ultimately resulting in findings and recommendations that are limited to the agricultural sector or to some kind of regulation of financial markets, as if this could protect the agricultural sector from its connection with the economic cycle of accumulation and from the broader framework of neoliberal policies, which have shrunk the traditional functions of the nation-state.

In this context, TAMs have engaged in negotiations with governments and the private sector to confront neoliberal policies without having an explicit analytical framework to drive the *institutional guerrilla* strategy that was supposed to use the entry points of policy dialogue and normative work at the institutional level to provide support to national and local struggles. Thus, I started to research the connection between the collapse of the Bretton Woods agreements and neoliberal policies in agriculture to better understand the ongoing financialization of agriculture and to read the ongoing negotiations at the FAO level within a broader framework.

This broader framework sheds a different light on what was at stake in the FAO policy dialogues on agroecology and biotechnologies for family farming under José Graziano da Silva's two terms as FAO director-general from 2011 to 2019. In this period, the most relevant negotiations occurred through the FAO International Year of Family Farming (2014), the FAO agro-ecology symposia (2014–18), and the FAO symposia on biotechnologies, innovation, and digitalization (2016–19). TAMs took part in negotiations of FAO policy frameworks (through the facilitation of the IPC) based on a common agenda promoting agroecology (IPC 2015) as a pathway toward the realization of food sovereignty and the transformation of the food system. These FAO negotiations resulted in the recognition of family farming and agroecology.

In response, the corporate sector sought to co-opt the focus on family farming and agroecology, using the new biotechnologies as a Trojan horse to appropriate the biodiversity at the core of family farming. Through the regulation of genetic information referred to as digital sequence information (DSI), and the production of plant varieties through the new breeding techniques (NBTs), industry could patent genes without distinguishing them from naturally occurring genes found in peasants' seeds, such that the entire crop biodiversity would be brought under the control of a few multinationals. In the FAO and Committee on World Food Security, TAMs' attempts to discuss seeds and genetic resources were blocked by a few governments referring to the jurisdiction of the WTO's Agreement on Trade-Related Aspects of Intellectual Property Rights (TRIPS).

Only through a broader theoretical lens referring to world-systems theory (Giovanni Arrighi, Jason W. Moore), international critical agrarian studies (Marc Edelman and Saturnino M. Borras Jr.), and nonterritorial governance approach (William Coleman) can the negotiations over the appropriation and patenting of seeds and biodiversity through NBTs and DSI be understood, not just as a casual phenomenon but as a strategic step in the current stage of capitalist development and the continuation of the existing hegemony. Indeed, seeds and biodiversity are central to the definition of the model of agriculture and the autonomy of peasant agriculture. The introduction of external inputs makes farming more dependent on agribusiness practices and capital-intensive approaches. In fact, the industrial agriculture model depends on the intensive use of resources, including industrial seeds and fertilizers produced with fossil fuels (Clapp 2017).

This explains the ongoing concentration in the agricultural inputs market: the nexus of seed and agrochemical corporations offering farm packages of seeds and pesticides, the creation of new products, the technological development related to digital farming platforms, the dematerialization of genetic resources (i.e., DSI) as big data become increasingly important for farming, and the high fixed costs of research and development (Clapp 2017; OECD 2018). It also explains the private sector's rationale for using the FAO normative processes to overrule the definition of living modified organisms in the Cartagena Protocol on Biosafety, and for considering plant varieties resulting from NBTS as not genetically modified organisms (GMOs) to generate a new policy framework and move beyond all the conflicts that blocked the old GMOs from fully penetrating the European market (Peschard and Randeria 2019). Building on the FAO discussions, the seed industry is concentrating its efforts on public policies and regulation, seeking homogenous regulation of NBTS across countries in order to eliminate the need for different products and thus reduce costs.

The broader theoretical framework composed of the three tiers of world-systems theory, international critical agrarian studies, and nonterritorial governance approach reads the inclusion of NBTS and DSI in agroecology as a way of expanding the external agroecological frontier (Webb 1964) and including all of the world's biodiversity in the capital accumulation system. The corporate sector's goal is further capital penetration into peasant agriculture to lower the costs of food production by dispossessing peasant farmers of natural resources and to shift capital accumulation to a new phase of material expansion (Moore 2010a, 2010b; Smith 2007). At the same time, this is part of an attempt to resolve the conflict between intellectual property rights and collective rights in the global governance of agriculture in favour of intellectual property rights through the appropriation of world biodiversity as a constitutive base of collective rights and agroecology.

This book focuses on the financialization of agriculture, which after the end of the Bretton Woods system reshaped the global governance space for agriculture, leading to the emergence of new TAMs. In particular, I look at how policy negotiations in recent years are defining the pathway of a new material expansion of the economy based on agroecology (labour intensive) or biotechnologies (capital intensive). Chapter 1 explores the literature to reach a definition of financialization, which in Chapter 2 is applied to agriculture. Chapter 3 describes the global governance of agriculture in relation to the hegemonic cycles of capital accumulation and the emergence of new TAMS supporting food sovereignty in the post–Bretton Woods financialization phase. Chapter 4 analyzes the clash over seeds and biodiversity in the global governance space, as hegemonic powers aim to achieve further capital penetration in peasant agriculture to shift to a new phase of capital accumulation based on material expansion. Chapter 5 draws some conclusions on TAMS' work to reshape the contested space of global governance of agriculture.

In order to redefine the political framework and the historical process, I have used official FAO documents, the IPC archive — housed at Centro Internazionale Crocevia, a Rome-based nongovernmental organization (NGO) in charge of the IPC secretariat — documents and articles published on the websites of CSOs, and academic literature. This book has been greatly informed by my position as general coordinator of the IPC secretariat in Rome from 2011 to 2020 and my experience supporting the efforts and strategies of TAMS in the FAO, working to realize the food sovereignty agenda, managing daily liaisons with the FAO Partnership Office, and reporting to the cabinet of the FAO director-general.

① Financialization and Capital Accumulation

> The real barrier of capitalist production is capital itself. (Marx 1967 III: 250)

In the last decades, "financialization" has become a buzzword. The 2008 subprime financial crisis generated a revival of interest in financial capital as the dominant actor in the economy, though financial crises have recurred at the global and local levels since the end of the Bretton Woods system. The first use of the term "financialization" can be traced back to Phillips (1993: 197), who defined it as "a prolonged split between the divergent real and financial economies":

> Finance cannot nurture a [large middle] class, because only a small elite portion of any national population — Dutch, British or American — can share in the profits of the bourse, merchant bank and countinghouse. Manufacturing, transportation and trade supremacies, by contrast, provide a broader national prosperity in which the ordinary person can man the production lines, mines, mills, wheels, mainsails and nets. Once this stage of economic development yields to the next, with its sharper divisions from capital, skills and education, great middle-class societies lose something vital and unique.

The financialization renaissance started with publications by Epstein (2005) and Krippner (2005). The ensuing proliferation of studies on financialization, with different approaches simplifying the topic or focusing on some particular micro aspects of contemporary capitalism, led Braga (2013) to describe the field as a Tower of Babel. According to Epstein (2005: 3), financialization can be defined by "the increasing role of financial motives, financial markets, financial actors and financial institutions in the operation of the domestic and international economies." Krippner (2005: 174), on the other hand, defines financialization as "the tendency for profit making in the economy to occur increasingly through financial channels rather than through productive activities," based on Arrighi's (1994: 6) definition where after a phase of material expansion, "money capital 'sets in motion' an increasing mass of commodities (including commoditized labor-power and gifts of nature); and in phases of financial expansion an expanded mass of money capital 'sets itself free' from its commodity form, and accumulation proceeds through financial deals (as in Marx's abridged formula M-M')." Epstein's and Krippner's definitions mark the two main positions of the debate on financialization — an increasing presence of financial agents in the economy for Epstein versus a divide between production and finance in capital accumulation for Krippner — even if the increasing divergence between the real and financial economy is perceived as a moment of crisis and instability in the economic system in both Epstein's and Krippner's work.

Epstein (2005) reviewed the literature on financialization to present historical and empirical evidence regarding how financialization has contributed to economic instability, inequalities, and declining productive investments and employment. The emergence of finance polarizes classes and favours the class of rentiers, supported by the deregulation of financial markets, which affects exchange rates, and by international trade, which invalidates the theory of comparative advantage. Therefore, financial liberalization and open capital markets influence economic crises in developing countries, with financial speculation dominating corporate policies. Epstein has no vision on the future development of the financialization process, but he urges some kind of regulation on financial transactions based on the Tobin tax. Thus, he follows a Keynesian approach, which aims to regulate the excess of capital mobility at the international level in order to fund public projects and investments.

Following the definition of financialization proposed by Epstein, Kotz (2008, 2015) asserts that neoliberalism is the most useful characterization of post-1980 capitalism, rather than financialization and globalization, which are just outcomes of the neoliberal context. In his view, neoliberalism is a coherent system of economic, social, and political institutions defining capital-labour relations. Kotz does not explain the root causes of the policy shift from Keynesianism to neoliberalism after the end of Bretton Woods, and just assumes that the latter is a new form of capitalism that emerged from the crisis of the previous one. Neoliberalism includes liberalization, privatization, and stabilization as means to transform the institutions of regulated capitalism into institutions of neoliberal capitalism, while financialization emerged in the 2000s as a phenomenon driven by neoliberal restructuring. Therefore, in Kotz's analysis, financialization is a consequence of neoliberalism; he does not provide an adequate overall framework to understand the development of capitalism in this period.

Kotz's nonexplicatory conclusions derive from the fact that he assumes Epstein's (2005) definition of financialization as the increasing presence of the financial sector in the economy, which involves neither a political imprinting of the phenomenon nor a clear understanding of the role of finance in the shift from Keynesian Fordism to the neoliberal age. Indeed, Epstein (2015: 5) himself describes his definition as "agnostic on the issue of whether it constitutes a new mode of accumulation or broadly characterizes an entire new phase of capitalism." Kotz's analysis assumes that the shift is a matter of fact, without identifying any root causes leading to the end of the Bretton Woods system, and financialization, as defined by Epstein, assumes a minor role.

Among those who think that financialization causes prolonged stagnation of the real economy, and not the other way around, Palley (2007, 2013) observes that financialization transforms the functioning of the economic system at the macro and micro levels. In particular, he concludes that "the business cycle generated by financialization may be unstable and end in prolonged stagnation" (Palley 2007: 26). Financialization implies low wages (no trickle-down effect) and increasing inequality in incomes, creating the conditions for stagnation and recession through an increased risk of debt deflation. Palley (2007, 2013) has identified flaws in the economic theory that justifies financialization and has developed an alternative theoretical approach and set of policies to restore full employment and replace the current corporate globalization with more equitable globalization based on policy dialogue. He suggests replacing the lack of government presence with a progressive "better government" agenda that would restore policy control over financial markets and challenge neoliberal policies, thus strengthening political processes and reducing the influence of corporations.

Along the same lines as Palley (2007), Orhangazi (2007) argues that financialization has a negative impact on investments due to (a) an investment increase in financial assets rather than real assets, which generates a crowding-in effect over real investments, and (b) the adoption of shareholder wealth maximization management at the corporate level, which pressures nonfinancial corporations to increase payments to financial markets in the form of dividends. Therefore, in Orhangazi's analysis too, the stagnation of the real economy is not a cause (as in the stagnation thesis) but an effect (as in the financialization thesis). Both Palley and Orhangazi aim to regulate the financial system to make it more equitable.

Krippner (2005) focuses on whether financialization is a fact: the analysis of shareholder value (Fligstein 1990) and the increase in new financial tools (Sassen 2001) do not allow for a full understanding of the relevance of the financialization process for the economic cycle. Krippner shows that the share of financial revenues on productive profits for nonfinancial firms has been increasing since the 1970s and has been led by the manufacturing sector (see Figure 1.1). This makes clear that financialization is a relevant trend of the economy in general, rather than of the postindustrial economy, and a useful concept to shed light on the connections between globalization, neoliberalism, and postindustrialism.

On the basis of data available from World War II onward, Krippner does not take a stand on the novelty of the financialization phase or on the persistence of the current phase. She sticks to the available quantitative data in order to promote an approach based on data checks, even if she recognizes the explanatory power of the historical approach used by Arrighi, who analyzes financialization over a *longue durée* from the sixteenth century. Indeed, Krippner's (2005) definition, taken from Arrighi (1994), focuses on forms of capital accumulation, which in turn originate from the overaccumulation and fall of the rate of profit. Krippner, Lemoine, and Ravelli (2017) quote Arrighi and Silver's (1999) analysis as a theoretical

Figure 1.1 Corporate Profits, 1959–2007

Source: Council of Economic Advisers (2008)

reference, limiting her research to verifying with data the current phase of financialization. Krippner (2005) focuses on only the quantitative analysis of the current phase, without entering into a broader theoretical analysis.

So in order to better understand Krippner's explanatory approach, we can deepen the complex approach of Arrighi (1994: 6), who defines financialization as an increasing mass of "money capital setting itself free from its commodity form," with capital accumulation proceeding through financial deals. This definition complements Krippner's definition thanks to two main contributions: (a) the application of Marx's formula M-M´ to the accumulation cycle and (b) the liberation of capital from its commodity form, and therefore from the need for this to go through a production process. When Arrighi (1994: 241) speaks about financialization, he refers clearly to a hegemonic power that lends money and provides liquidity for the whole system rather than investing in trade:

> For one thing, their switch from trade to finance can be taken as the clearest sign that the time to bring trade expansion to an end in order to prevent it from destroying profitability had *really* come. Moreover, the agencies in question were better positioned than any other to monitor and act on the *overall* tendencies of the capitalist world-economy, that is, to act as intermediaries and regulators of the expanding supply of, and demand for, money capital.

Distinct from other narratives, in Arrighi's work the financial agencies stabilize the world-system and foster a financial expansion that secures profits: these agencies are not the cause of systemic instability, they just react to the instability of the system to generate profits through finance.

In brief, the financial expansion is the key moment in the concentration of capital, transforming the end of a cycle of accumulation into the beginning of a new cycle. Indeed, in the financialization phase, two different kinds of capital accumulation take place in parallel: the first capital accumulation occurs within the dominant regime of accumulation, while the second capital accumulation occurs within regional structures of accumulation that destabilize the old regime and foreshadow the emergence of a new phase of material expansion of the capitalist world economy.

According to Arrighi (1994) and Arrighi and Silver (1999), the current phase of financialization derives from the end of the Bretton Woods agreements, which can be traced back to the crisis of the three pillars of the U.S hegemony of capital accumulation that started after World War II. The three pillars were (a) a publicly regulated dollar system, which gave the U.S.

government effective control over global liquidity and enabled the promotion of a generalized expansion of world trade that saw few precedents in capitalist history; (b) the General Agreement on Tariffs and Trade (GATT), the United Nations, and Bretton Woods, which were meant to govern the formation of a world market under the control of the U.S. government, and, in particular, defined the pace and direction of trade liberalization; and (c) transnational corporations (TNCs), which integrated mass production and mass distribution processes within a single organization by internalizing a whole sequence of subprocesses (from the procurement of primary inputs to the disposal of final outputs) and growing proportions of world trade into giant and vertically integrated domestic business organizations, so as to control foreign direct investment (the main tool of post-World War II reconstruction) and shift managerial control of substantial sectors of foreign economies to U.S. nationals: "US corporations began to move to foreign countries almost as soon as they had completed their continent-wide integration.... In becoming national firms, US corporations learned how to become international" (Hymer 1972 in Arrighi 1994: 249). Arrighi (1994: 249–50) writes, "The spectacular domestic and trans-statal expansion of US multi-unit, vertically integrated business enterprises, and the organizational barriers to entry which they created were associated with an equally spectacular growth of managerial hierarchies and bureaucratic structures. Once in place, these hierarchies and structures themselves 'became a source of permanence, power and continued growth.'"

So by the end of the Bretton Woods agreements, TNCs were embedded in a global system of production, exchange, and accumulation independent from any state authority. The contradiction between the domestic foundations of U.S. power and the expansion of U.S. corporations abroad (including in the Eurocurrency market) shifted the control of liquidity back from Washington to London and New York. According to Arrighi, the economic crisis of the 1970s originated from the end of the gold-dollar exchange standard defined by the Bretton Woods agreements and by the oil shocks. In fact, the end of the Bretton Woods agreements started between 1968 and 1973, with the explosion of the Eurodollar market. The Eurodollar market was an unplanned outcome of the U.S. regime of accumulation: TNCs were the most important depositors of the U.S. currency market, and U.S. banks naturally had access to offshore banking (and controlled 50 percent of it by 1961) due to the greater freedom of movement that this affords. The U.S. surplus in the balance of payments and large gold reserves supported the expansion of U.S. corporate capital and the role of the dollar as a global currency. At the end of the 1960s, the London-centred Eurodollar market exponentially increased its liquidity. The speculation on the regime of fixed exchange rates made the fiction of the gold-dollar exchange standard unsustainable, with U.S. gold reserves already falling short due to the action of foreign governments. The U.S. Federal Reserve could not address the increasing speculation: the floating exchange rate left it to markets to fix the price of national currencies and regulate the balance between the U.S. current account surpluses that financed the U.S. capital account deficit. Other countries, which under the fixed exchange rate had to keep their balance of payments in some sort of equilibrium, could now borrow from the market due to the infinite availability of liquidity, without adjustments to higher oil prices and with increasing inflation worldwide. Moreover, corporate capital had to protect itself from the day-to-day exchange rate fluctuations of the currencies in which their assets were quoted (Arrighi 2007; Arrighi and Silver 1999; Braga 2013; Foster 2008; Sweezy 1997).

Indeed, offshore deposits accumulated world liquidity outside of the control of governments, which in turn were trying, unsuccessfully, to counteract such concentration by manipulating the exchange rates of their currencies and interest rates. The continuous fluctuation of the exchange rate and the rate of interest differentials increased speculation and trade opportunities in money markets for offshore capital. By the mid-1970s monetary transactions in offshore money markets exceeded the value of world trade many times over (eleven times in 1979, twenty times in 1987). The financial expansion became unstoppable, and the financial expansion of U.S. hegemony became a core aspect of the end of Bretton Woods (Arrighi and Silver 1999; Braga 2013).

The context in which this financial phase started, according to Arrighi, included an inelastic supply of labourers and primary products (as well as rising pressure on prices). This created an accumulation of capital that, instead of increasing "world trade and production as it had done in the 1950s and early 1960s, resulted in world-wide cost inflation and a massive flight of capital to offshore money markets" (Arrighi 1994: 315). The so-called pay explosion from 1968 to 1973 was followed by an oil shock (the price grew threefold in 1974), producing an approximate $80 billion surplus of petrodollars and reducing any real trade profitability. The oil rent was reinvested in the Eurocurrency market, thus increasing free liquidity and financial speculation in offshore markets, where any regulatory attempt was destined to fail (Arrighi and Silver 1999; Braga 2013; Foster 2008; Krippner 2004).

Most of these petrodollars and Eurodollars reemerged through the banking system as competitors of the official U.S. dollars issued by the U.S.

government, to the detriment of both the U.S. government and businesses. Many countries accessed the liquidity without any constraint in the balance of payments, thus undermining the seigniorage privileges of the U.S. government. Concurrently, however, offshore money markets were invaded by more liquidity than could possibly be invested profitably. According to Arrighi, TNCs controlled the offshore money markets, rendered traditional national policies useless, and imposed serious constraints on the sovereignty of nation-states through the world-scale processes of production and exchange used by TNCs and the consolidation of suprastatal world markets. Ultimately, the sovereignty of nation-states shifted upward (through globalization and the increasing role of international, intergovernmental, and financial institutions), sideways (through the privatization of governance structures), and downward (through political and fiscal decentralization), as part of the so-called neoliberal reduction of the national state (Edelman and Borras 2016). Assuming the framework of Arrighi's world-systems theory, neoliberal policies (which can be traced back to monetarism) are the expression of the financialization phase of the current hegemonic cycle of accumulation.

Arrighi (1994, 2007) and Arrighi and Silver (1999) describe financialization as a recurrent outcome of a crisis of overaccumulation, in which capital cannot find opportunities for remunerative real investments. The result is an intensification of interstate and interenterprise competition, leading to the vertical and horizontal integration of enterprises, the extension of the proletarianization process, the polarization of society, the shrinking of the middle class, and ultimately the multiplication of social conflicts. Only the emergence of a new social bloc generating a change in hegemony will be able to tame social conflicts. However, according to Arrighi (1994: 239–40), financialization is just one of the two mutually exclusive paths of the capitalist process of accumulation, which by definition is contradictory and unstable, especially in its financial phase:

> This combination of circumstances leads some (mostly capitalist) agencies to divert their cash flows from the trading to the credit system, thereby increasing the supply of loanable funds, and other (mostly territorialist) agencies to seek through borrowing the additional financial resources needed to survive in the more competitive environment, thereby increasing the demand for loanable funds. It follows that the revenue-maximizing and profit-maximizing branches into which logistics of world economic expansion are assumed to bifurcate do not describe actual

trajectories. Rather, they describe a field of forces defined by the coexistence of two alternative and mutually exclusive ideotypical paths of capital accumulation, the unity and opposition of which is the source of turbulence and instability in the world system of trade and accumulation....

When the two paths bifurcate, in contrast, the logic of trade expansion and the logic of capital accumulation diverge; the accumulation of capital is no longer embedded in the expansion of the world-economy; and the pace of both processes not only slows down but becomes unstable.... The predisposition of capitalist organizations to withdraw cash surpluses from trade and production in response to falling profits and increasing risks, in contrast, continually tends to pull the mass of capital invested in commodities downwards, towards or below the lower path, so that the profits of trade and production rise and those of lending and speculation fall.

In short, when capital accumulation enters a (CM') phase of financial expansion its trajectory does not follow a steady path but becomes subject to more or less violent downswings and upswings which recreate and destroy over and over again the profitability of capital invested in trade.

The idea of cyclical financialization comes from Arrighi's reading of Braudel's Civilization and Capitalism trilogy, in which Braudel (1992) identifies historical phases of financialization of the capital accumulation process as recurrent: (a) in Italy in the fifteenth and sixteenth centuries, when Genoa withdrew from commercial activities to exercise financial power over Europe, (b) when the Dutch relinquished commerce around 1740 to turn into the "bankers of Europe," and (c) when the British, during the Great Depression of 1873–96, tried to allocate the money capital accumulated during the industrial revolution. Arrighi also includes in this cyclical trend the post-Fordism/Keynesianism neoliberal period starting in the 1970s. Braudel's intuition regarding the historical cycles of financial capital is elaborated by Arrighi in the framework of Marxist theory, with particular reference to the Marxist formula of capital M-C-M′ (where money is invested in a combination of inputs in order to produce an output commodity and generate an expanded liquidity) — not the logic of a single investment, but the logic of a full cycle of capital accumulation:

The central aspect of this pattern is the alternation of epochs of material expansion (MC phases of capital accumulation) with phases of financial rebirth and expansion (CM′ phases). In phases of material expansion money capital "sets in motion" an increasing mass of commodities (including commoditized labor-power and gifts of nature); and in phases of financial expansion an increasing mass of money capital "sets itself free" from its commodity form, and accumulation proceeds through financial deals (as in Marx's abridged formula MM′). Together, the two epochs or phases constitute a full *systemic cycle of accumulation* (MCM′). (Arrighi 1994: 6)

For Arrighi, financialization is just a recurrent phase of the crisis of capital accumulation in which the trickle-down effect of wealth to the working class, typical of commercial expansion, is suspended — as is social harmony under the hegemonic centre of capital accumulation. More specifically, the financialization phase prepares for a new commercial expansion under a novel regime of accumulation. First, financial expansion creates a new regime of accumulation that develops within the old regime. This is followed by a consolidated phase of material expansion of the new regime, which is then followed by a second financial expansion characterized by a new financial crisis. Each financial expansion is identified by a switch in the capital of the leading agency from trade and production to financial intermediation and speculation. This switch reveals a negative judgement on the possibility of continuing to profit from the reinvestment of surplus capital in the material expansion of the world economy, as well as a positive judgment on the possibility of prolonging in time and space the agency's dominance through a greater specialization in high finance.

Although it helps capital accumulation during the final part of the material expansion of the world economy, the financial phase has always been a preamble to a deepening crisis and to a new regime of accumulation overcoming the previously dominant one. The crucial part is the role played by business organizations since their organizational revolutions are central in Arrighi's analysis: any material expansion of the world economy has historically been based on a specific organizational structure that expanded itself as a successful model, progressively lost its capacity to innovate and to have higher returns, and ultimately gave way for new organizational innovations to be established. Interstate and interenterprise competition are based on imitation of the hegemonic business model, which brings down profit rates and pushes capital from trade to finance. In this phase, high competition and low profit rates cause salary reductions, creating phases of turbulence and chaos. Only when the new hegemonic power creates a new organizational form and business model does a new phase of commercial expansion begin. Therefore, Arrighi introduces organizational revolutions and innovations as key factors in the cycles of capital accumulation. Arrighi's (1994, 2007) and Arrighi and Silver's (1999) analyses share similarities with Foster's (2007, 2008) reading of Sweezy (1997), who identifies a new phase of capitalism in 1974–75 based on the decreasing rate of growth and the proliferation of TNCs, and sees the financialization of capital accumulation as the driving force that lifted economic growth in the 1970s. Using a previous analysis (Baran and Sweezy 1966), Sweezy understands financialization as the outcome of a monopoly capitalist economy, where a global productive system generates huge surpluses without having enough opportunities to invest them. According to him, the solution has been to create new financial markets with new financial products (such as derivatives and swaps) and money capital.

In part, this analysis is shared by Ghosh (2005, 2010, 2011), who analyzes the financial liberalization process with a particular focus on developing countries. Ghosh (2005) identifies the rise of financial liberalization with the end of Bretton Woods due to the fact that in the 1960s and '70s the international banking system, and the Eurocurrency market more specifically, was flooded with an excess of liquidity from the surpluses of oil-exporting countries. This excess liquidity was invested in developing countries through cross-border capital flows and foreign exchange convertibility. At the same time, governments withdrew from financial intermediation activities, while the banking system became completely privatized and stopped fostering growth in the real sector and development of the countries in which it operated. A major concern for Ghosh (2005, 2010) is how the outflows of capital generated by financial liberalization have been moving from developing countries to developed ones. Therefore, national and individual debts are part of Ghosh's analysis. She recommends a new social role for financial intermediation and the intervention of accountable states in the economy through regulation. Just one year before the financial crisis, in the 2006 *Global Financial Stability Report*, the International Monetary Fund (IMF) clearly presented its concerns regarding the deceleration of the real economy and the growth of financial derivatives.

The opposite thesis is supported by Foster (2007, 2008) and Foster and Magdoff (2014), who consider financialization an important aspect of the contemporary economy, transforming the monopoly capital described by Sweezy into monopoly-finance capital. Building on the perspectives of Marx and Keynes, Foster and Magdoff argue that capital accumulation has always been embedded as a possible contradiction between real accumulation (ownership of real assets) and financial speculation (paper claiming real assets). Monopoly capitalism has made this decoupling possible thanks to mature financial systems that can move beyond the simple financial bubbles of the past to an overlying financial structure dominating the stagnating production system. Since the 1980s, states too have been embedded in the system so as to avoid a further crisis for monopoly-finance capital. Foster and Magdoff follow the analysis of Sweezy, defining financialization as the response of the system to stagnation in order to maintain the generation of profits. Financialization played a clear role in lifting the economy after the end of Bretton Woods, as the deregulation of financial markets was aimed at expanding existing financial bubbles. Foster and Magdoff (2014) support Sweezy's proposal to expand public spending in support of populations and to radically redistribute income and wealth. They are aware that capital accumulation is the root cause of the financial crisis, and therefore they propose a global tax on capital as a possible solution to counter monopolistic accumulation.

Braga (2013) and Ferreira (2017) present a distinct analysis of financialization. They see the financialization process of capital as the development of capital in its most perfect and original form, moving beyond its own contradictions, such as Marx's value theory, and abstracting its own value determinations. This pure and original form of capital could lead to the vanishing of capitalism, making financialization the last stage of capitalist development. In this view, real accumulation is a previous stage, and financial accumulation a more evolved stage, with no possibility of reverting back.

The IMF's (2016) *Global Report on Financial Stability* confirms the excess of available capital, ruling out the hypothesis of financialization producing stagnation through a crowding-out effect. Differences among scholars supporting financialization as a response to stagnation concern the reversible nature of financialization (Foster and Magdoff 2014), financialization as the final stage of capitalism (Braga 2013; Ferreira 2017), and financialization as a cyclical phase (Arrighi 1994, 2007; Arrighi and Silver 1999). In general, the debate on financialization relates to multiple analyses of capitalism, financial markets, and financial speculation. Overall, we can conclude by identifying three main approaches:

1. *Microeconomic approach.* This approach is based on corporate governance and on the alignment between corporate managers and the maximization of utility for shareholders. Financialization is a side

effect of the management of the corporate business shifting corporate money-capital investments from production to financial circuits (Froud et al. 2000).

2. *Keynesian approach.* This approach focuses on financial institutions. The financialization process originates in financial speculative bubbles, and thus regulation of financial markets will mitigate the effects of financialization (Epstein 2005; Ghosh 2010; Palley 2007; Orhangazi 2007).

3. *Marxist approach.* This approach interprets financialization in relation to capitalist accumulation from multiple angles: financialization as the last perfect stage of capitalism (Braga 2013; Ferreira 2017); as the dominance of finance monopoly capital (Foster and Magdoff 2014), which can be changed only through an alliance of popular upsurges in the Global South (external proletariat) and in the developed world (internal proletariat); and as a cyclical phase of the capitalist accumulation cycle (Arrighi 1994, 2007; Arrighi and Silver 1999; Krippner 2005; Krippner, Lemoine, and Ravelli 2017).

The microeconomic approach does not provide any root causes for or problematize the current phase of financialization. Regarding Epstein's (2005) agnostic vision in the Keynesian approach, Krippner's (2005) analysis allows us to correctly highlight how Epstein's analysis focuses on a particular and specific manifestation of financialization without addressing the core of the process, despite Epstein's claim that his definition of financialization lacks specificity because it can include many features. Krippner's critique can be applied because Epstein's broad approach can include many financial actors in the economy but does not distinguish between financial actors investing in productive and trade processes (M-C-M′) and those investing just financially (M-M′). Therefore, even the Keynesian approaches, which support new regulations, do not ground their analyses in structural change to the conditions of capital accumulation. Assuming that the end of the Bretton Woods system originated in an excess of capital (overaccumulation), it is not clear how the Keynesian proposal for the reregulation of financial markets could change and reverse the conditions of capital accumulation.

The Marxist approach recognizes a structural shift after Bretton Woods (Arrighi 1994, 2007; Arrighi and Silver 1999; Braga 2013; Ferreira 2017; Kotz 2008, 2015) and provides the elements for analyses that can explain the subsequent process and emergence of TAMs. An exception is the approach developed by Braga (2013) and Ferreira (2017), which uses Baran and Sweezy's (1966) analysis of monopoly capital, assuming a more mature financial structure; however, this does not explain how the Bretton Woods agreements came to an end or the developments that followed. Arrighi provides the deepest analysis, connecting the different components of public money, TNCs, and global institutions with the cycle of capital accumulation, thus providing an exhaustive explanatory framework. Indeed, according to Arrighi (1994, 2007) and Arrighi and Silver (1999), the World Bank, the IMF, and the United Nations resurged in the 1980s and early 1990s as instruments to confront the unravelling hegemony of the United States in an increasingly chaotic world. For Arrighi, what in the Keynesian and other Marxist analyses is called "financial structure" is deeply related to state power, the privatization of money through TNCs, and the role that the IMF, the World Bank, and the United Nations play in a framework linked to the cycle of capital accumulation.

The U.S. government had sought to control the formation of a world market through the 1947 establishment of the GATT, according to Arrighi. Trade liberalization was left in the hands of national governments, and negotiations to lower tariffs were reduced to bilateral and multilateral agreements. U.S. president Franklin D. Roosevelt had previously tried to institutionalize the idea of a United Nations world government in order to manage the process of decolonization and guarantee the self-determination of each national community, which would participate on an equal footing in the United Nations General Assembly. Roosevelt's idea of a world government encompassing the globe was overcome by subsequent U.S. president Harry S. Truman's "free-worldism," which established a Cold War world order in which the United States replaced the United Nations in world-system governance based on the control of world money and military power. Supplementary support came from Bretton Woods institutions such as the IMF, the World Bank, and the United Nations, which supported U.S. policies or were impeded from functioning. Indeed, until the 1970s the U.S. Federal Reserve System played a major role, compared to the IMF and the World Bank, in the regulation of world money. Only with the crisis of U.S. hegemony in the 1970s and especially in the 1980s did the Bretton Woods organizations for the first time rise to prominence in the system of global monetary regulation.

By looking at the connections between the different levels of analysis, the Arrighi framework examines and comprehends financialization — as confirmed by Krippner's (2005) quantitative analysis for the period after World War II and by Fasianos, Diego, and Christos (2016) for the entire twentieth century — especially by addressing the evolution of global governance from the end of Bretton Woods to the United Nations and the WTO, when the material phase of accumulation hit a crisis point. Financialization through neoliberal policies generated a new space of global governance (in particular in regard to agriculture), and the new TAMs that emerged as a consequence have been using this space of global governance to confront the neoliberal policies that generated it. Such a connection sits at the core of this book, considering that Arrighi does not clearly elaborate on the role of transnational movements in the analysis of financialization. I return to this point regarding TAMs in the conclusion, with a focus on the role of class struggle and the revolutionary subject in hegemonic change. Arrighi and Silver (1999), however, refer to Markoff (1996) and Tilly (1995) in regard to the necessity of recreating some form of democratic transnational decision-making in the emerging world through transnational movements capable of extracting "concessions from the new holders of transnational power" (Markoff 1996: 132–35). Tilly (1995: 22) concurs but is more pessimistic, at least in the short run, about whether this will happen.

2 Globalization, Capital Accumulation, and the Role of Agriculture

> Material and financial expansions are both processes of a system of accumulation and rule that has increased in scale and scope over the centuries but has encompassed from its earliest beginnings a large number and variety of governmental and business agencies. Within each cycle, material expansions occur because of the emergence of a particular bloc of governmental and business agencies capable of leading the system towards a new spatial fix that creates the conditions for the emergence of wider or deeper divisions of labor. (Arrighi 2007: 231)

In the first chapter, I explained why I consider the most appropriate definition of financialization to be the phenomenon that occurs when an "increasing mass of money capital 'sets itself free' from its commodity form, and accumulation proceeds through financial deals" (Arrighi 1994: 6). In order to apply this definition of financialization to agriculture — and given that the specificity of financialization of agriculture has not been discussed extensively — I assume as a starting point the most relevant work developed after the 2007–08 food crisis, which is that by Isakson (2014, 2015) and Clapp (2014a, 2014b), first individually and more recently together (Clapp and Isakson 2018a, 2018b; Clapp, Isakson, and Visser 2016). They assume Epstein's (2005: 3) agnostic definition of financialization: "the increasing role of financial motives, financial markets, financial actors and financial institutions in the operation of the domestic and international economies." As we saw in the previous chapter, this definition focuses on the nature of the agents rather than on the nature of the investments (M-M′).

According to Isakson and Clapp, the process of financialization contributes in several ways to what they define as *distancing*. First of all, financialization "abstracts food from its physical form into highly complex agricultural commodity 'derivatives' that only seasoned financial traders fully understand" (Clapp 2012a: 2; Clapp 2014a, 2014b; Clapp, Isakson, and Visser 2016; Isakson 2014). Moreover, the financialization process has increased the number of actors and steps involved in global commodity value chains. In this context of *distancing*, the capacity of farmer organizations to influence the agri-food sector decreases, and it is difficult to distinguish the agricultural sector from the financial sector, and the activities related to real investments from the activities connected to financial investments, including the difference between hedging and financial speculation in agricultural commodity markets (Clapp, Isakson, and Visser 2016).

In her work, Clapp (2012b, 2017) refers to neoliberal policies and structural adjustment programs as key to the redefinition of agricultural policies, in light of the withdrawal of state support for agriculture and of the World Bank's and IMF's support for the liberalization of agricultural markets so as to allow developing countries to pay their debt. More specifically, Clapp (2012b: 59) refers to "enormous levels of external debt in the early 1980s as a result of global economic conditions that prevailed in the 1970s." In their joint work, Clapp and Isakson do not further develop the analysis of global economic conditions; indeed, in *Speculative Harvests*, Clapp and Isakson (2018b) assume that the beginning of the financialization process can be traced to the 1970s, neoliberal policies, and the deregulation of financial markets, and that the increasing role of financial actors in agriculture has been allowed due to the decreasing presence of the state and public support for agriculture. They focus on ongoing processes of financialization to ultimately define what financialization means at the concrete level, arguing that the financialization of agriculture has three main characteristics, which overlap, mutually reinforce one another, and directly challenge systems of food security and livelihoods and foster food price volatility, land-grabbing, and corporate concentration:

1. *The opening of new financial arenas*. After the U.S. government passed the Commodity Futures Modernization Act in 2000, the deregulation of financial markets allowed financial investors to differentiate their portfolios. This led to the creation of new financial tools linked to food and agriculture as commodity index funds, as well as other financial products with innovative mechanisms for connecting smallholders in "emerging" economies to financial markets (e.g., weather-based derivatives as a means of hedging against environmental risks).

2. *The prioritization of shareholder value*. This corresponds to short-termism in corporate investment policies, which encourages mergers

and acquisitions to increase market share and reduce duplicated costs (e.g., research and development), leads to lower wages and environmental standards, increases profits, and results in shareholders being paid higher dividends.

3. *The financialization of everyday life.* This leads farmers to access credit through private institutions instead of public ones, individualizing the cost of failures and enabling financial services to control and shape the retail sector and consumers.

Financial investments in agricultural commodities and commodity index funds are undertaken under the logic of portfolio differentiation and were at the root of the food price crisis and volatility of 2007–08. The increasing presence of the financial sector (equity funds, pension funds, banks, etc.) is considered an indicator of financialization itself (Clapp and Isakson 2018b). Therefore, the analysis is not limited to the financialization of the supply chain, the strengthening of the retail sector (Isakson 2014), and the transformation of farmland as a financial asset: it is extended to the financialization of the whole food system. As an example, the creation of new financial tools and collateral assets related to productive activities strengthens the agri-food sector's capacity to limit small-scale food producers' access to credit and markets. In addition, the prioritization of shareholder value increases short-term profitability (e.g., capital gains) through the restructuring of the sector (especially retail), creating more dependence on private credit rather than encouraging long-term investment in the agri-food sector. The outcome of this is that TNCs and financial actors extract wealth from the agricultural sector at the expense of farmers and consumers — who in turn pay the costs of this restructuring — and impede collective and political action thanks to the opacity and distance of the financial system.

Clapp and Isakson's (2018b) main conclusion is that financialization generates inequalities in the food system and compromises its socioecological resilience capacity to resist due to the opacity and abstract nature of such financialization. In their latest extensive work, *Speculative Harvests*, they offer three main recommendations: (a) research and better understand the financialization of agriculture in order to nurture public discussion about its effects on agriculture, (b) recognize the key role of CSOs in strategizing how to take on nation-states and global governance mechanisms so as to include bottom-up solutions in national and international levels of regulation, and (c) build alternative food systems with small-scale and ecological producers, unaffected by financialization. Vander Stichele (2014: 11) summarizes

Clapp and Isakson's discourse on the regulation of financial markets as follows: "So far, the focus of financial regulators and supervisors has been almost exclusively on financial stability. No financial reform or regulation has held the financial sector responsible for the impact of its financial activities on the economy, the society and the environment."

Clapp and Isakson, whose work can be considered the benchmark for research on the financialization of agriculture, assume as a starting point the agnostic definition of financialization developed by Epstein (2005, 2015). Epstein asserts that the financialization process has a negative impact on the economy and society, but he does not provide any specific recommendations on how to regulate financial markets. His conclusion is simply that "there's something happening here" (Epstein 2015: 14) and it is necessary to intervene somehow. Epstein arrives at a Keynesian conclusion, but he does not develop a deep Keynesian analysis of the causes of financialization. In a similar mode, Clapp and Isakson (2018b) conclude by acknowledging the need to develop further research on financialization. They connect multiple instances and historical periods when financialization emerged, but they do identify its root causes. They include among the main characteristics of financialization the neoclassical/mainstream approach on shareholder value, which defines financialization at the level of corporate policies, and the search for new financial arenas, which is usually linked to overaccumulation (although they do not mention this link). Both characteristics could be theoretically explained by the fall of profit rates: corporate investments are not made with the expectation of long-term returns, and they are therefore diversified when it comes to the creation of new markets for financial investment.

The preference given to financial investments rather than productive ones in the financialization process is not clearly discussed by Clapp and Isakson. This may be the most precarious point of their analysis, since it is not possible to identify whether the current dominance of financial investments is due to the deregulation of financial markets in the last decades, or the fact that investing in production and trade is no longer profitable. In the first scenario, the flow of investments in production and trade until the 1970s and 1980s would have resulted from the strict financial regulation of national states (Martin and Clapp 2015). Current regulation, too, would have resulted from a political choice made by national governments, creating the conditions for ongoing financialization. In order to better understand the issue, we can refer to analyses of mergers and acquisitions in the food sector, which, according to Clapp (2012) and Isakson (2014), occur as companies pursue the maximization of shareholder value.

In *Bigger Is Not Always Better*, Clapp (2017) offers a detailed examination of mergers and acquisitions in food and agriculture, coming to the same conclusion she developed in the studies with Isakson: the increasing number of mergers and acquisitions is an outcome of the prioritization of shareholder value in the financialization process. Her work is in line with Isakson's (2014) study, explaining how mergers and acquisitions in the food sector are driven by the poor financial performance of the Big Six — Monsanto, Bayer, DuPont, Dow, Syngenta, and BASF — and their competing strategies to vertically integrate their business. The Big Six are the result of a previous process of mergers and acquisitions among big chemical, pharmaceutical, and seed companies as well as other small seed and biotech companies in the 1990s and early 2000s. The expected outcome of the newly born Big Six was the full integration of biotech companies with pharmaceuticals, seeds, and agricultural chemicals. At that point, Monsanto was an American multinational agrochemical and agricultural biotechnology conglomerate known for producing GM seeds; Bayer was a German multinational life sciences, pharmaceutical, and chemical company; DuPont was an American chemicals company involved in agriculture, biobased materials, advanced materials, and electronics; Dow was an American multinational chemical conglomerate developing products for agriculture, automotive, construction, and other industrial markets; Syngenta was a Swiss agricultural company producing seeds and agrochemicals; and BASF was a German chemical company and the largest chemical producer in the world with subsidiaries and joint ventures in more than eighty countries. In 2017 and 2018 the acquisitions of Syngenta by ChemChina and Monsanto by Bayer, plus the merger of Dow and Dupont, were finalized, leading to further concentration in the agricultural inputs market (see Table 2.1).

Clapp (2017) considers the weak agricultural commodity prices since 2013 to be the reason for low demand for agricultural inputs, which, according to the Big Six (Zhang 2017), was the main impetus for the mergers within the seed industry. Figure 2.1 indicates the price depression of global farm products, and Figure 2.2 shows the relative increasing prices of agricultural inputs compared to farm commodities, which resulted in the poor financial performance of the Big Six. In addition, Clapp (2017) mentions the strategic reasons for vertical integration: the nexus of seed and agrochemical corporations offering farm packages for seeds and pesticides, the creation of new products, the technological development related to digital farming platforms, the dematerialization of genetic resources (DSI) as big data become increasingly important for farming, and access to plant genetic material. Even while recognizing the above-mentioned factors as

Table 2.1 Big Six Mergers and Acquisitions

Company	Bayer	Monsanto	Dow	Dupont	ChemChina	Syngenta	BASF
Size of deal	$66bn (acquisition)		$130bn (merger)		$43bn (acquisition)		N.A.
Sales (2015)	€46.3bn	US$15bn	US$49bn	US$25bn	US$45bn	US$13,4bn	€70.4bn
Employees	116,800	20,000+	53,000	52,000	140,000	28,704	112,435
Country	Germany	US$15bn	US$49bn	US	China	Switzerland	Germany
% of Global Seed Market in 2013	3%	26%	4%	21%	N.A.	8%	N.A.
% of Global Pesticide Market in 2013	18%	8%	10%	6%	N.A.	20%	13%

Source: ETC Group (2015)

Figure 2.1 Cereals Price Index

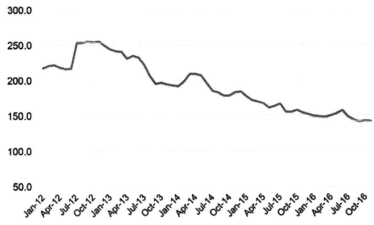

Source: FAO Agricultural Market Information System

Figure 2.2 Agricultural Input Prices

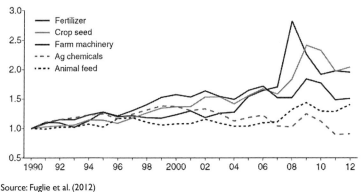

Source: Fuglie et al. (2012)

leading to the concentration of the agricultural sector (see Table 2.2), in her analysis these trends also lead to the maximization of shareholder value, considering that a few institutional investors, such as BlackRock (see Table 2.3), control part of the equity capital of the Big Six through asset managers that have incentives based on short-term investment performance, including the return on equity based on a short-term period.

"It was in this broader context that shareholder pressure came down on agribusiness for companies to improve their returns, including pressure to restructure as a means to save costs and shore up profits," states Clapp

Table 2.2 Driving Factors for Market Concentration in Agricultural Input

Factors driving changes in market structure varied by industry	
Farm input sector	Factor driving consolidation and concentration
Crop seed and bio-technology	Acquisition of complementary technology and marketing assets, economies of scale in crop biotechnology research and development (R&D)
Agricultural chemicals	Stricter environmental and safety regulations; maturing markets; rise of generic products
Farm machinery	Financial losses of major manufacturers during farm-sector business cycles (which strongly influence demand for large capital purchases)
Animal breeding and genetics	Vertical integration of poultry and livestock industries; economies of scale in animal biotechnology R&D
Animal health	Spillover from consolidation in the human pharma-ceutical industry, which is being driven by loss of profit streams and idled capacity when major drugs go off-patent

Source: Fuglie et al. (2012)

(2017: 16). This passage clarifies how the analysis of financialization can differ radically depending on whether we apply Epstein's (2005) definition of financialization — that is, an increasing presence of financial actors — or the definition developed by Arrighi (1994: 372) and assumed by Krippner (2005: 181) — that is, "the tendency for profit making in the economy to occur increasingly through financial channels rather than through productive activities." The fact that the actors involved in the restructuring were financial firms is relevant for Epstein but insignificant for Arrighi and Krippner, since the restructuring and mergers and acquisitions were aimed at increasing the returns of the companies (Clapp 2017), which simply equates to an improvement in their productive activities.

Figure 2.3 confirms that the acquisitions were production oriented, showing how the new acquisitions have increased the growth of sales of the top four firms, which, in turn, have witnessed lower than average growth in each agricultural input sector. This proves that there are decreasing returns for the biggest firms that follow a horizontal and vertical integration strategy. Indeed, an IPES-Food (2017: 5) report on market concentration concludes that "the scope of research and innovation has narrowed as dominant firms

Table 2.3 Percentage of Shares Held in the Big Six by Large Asset Management Firms

	Monsanto %	Bayer %	Dow %	DuPont %	Syngenta %	BASF %
BlackRock	5.76	10.09	6.11	6.61	6.00	8.30
Capital Group	2.68	3.68	3.60	10.69	4.01	0.91
Fidelity	3.12	1.71	1.17	3.54	0.21	0.50
The Vanguard Group, Inc	7.33	2.30	6.27	6.87	2.28	2.31
State Street Global Advisors	4.63	0.50	4.14	5.01	0.40	0.45
Norges Bank Investment Management (NBIM)	0.81	1.64	0.43	0.63	1.75	3.00
Owned by the Top 6 firms before mergers	24.33	19.92	21.72	33.35	14.65	15.47

Source: Clapp (2017)

Figure 2.3 Market Concentration, 1994–2009

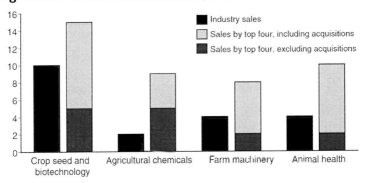

Source: Fuglie et al. (2012)

have bought out the innovators and shifted resources to more defensive modes of investment."

The Organisation for Economic Cooperation and Development (OECD 2018: 13) too shows that consolidation in global seeds markets depends on the high fixed costs of research and development, which leads to a push for horizontal mergers and acquisitions, and the complementarities between seeds, biotechnology, chemicals, and precision agriculture, which lead to a push for nonhorizontal integration:

Consolidation in global seed markets has been ongoing for several decades and has two main causes. High fixed costs, in particular for R&D [research and development], create pressure for "horizontal" mergers that combine firms with activities in the same domains. In parallel, technological and commercial complementarities between seeds, GM technology, and crop protection chemicals create incentives for "non-horizontal" mergers between companies active in these different domains. A new complementarity may be emerging today with digital technologies and precision agriculture. Major seed and crop protection companies have been investing in digital agriculture in recent years, as big data could enable customised advice to farmers on the best seeds or crop protection products to use and could in turn inform R&D.

Clapp's (2017) reading of the poor financial performance and the strategic motives for concentration driving mergers and acquisitions among the Big Six does not allow for concluding that shareholder value is the driving factor in financialization.

On the contrary, the trend toward vertical and horizontal concentration (see Figures 2.3 and Figure 2.4) shows the decreasing rate of profit (Figures 2.1 and 2.2) in a mature economy (see Table 2.4) in which big corporations control markets with a low rate of growth while sitting on a *large pile of cash* (Clapp 2017), since there are no profitable opportunities for real investments. IPES-Food (2017: 5) supports this vision of a "significant horizontal and vertical restructuring ... across food systems," led by the emergence of new data technologies as a powerful new driver of consolidation to control

Figure 2.4 Mergers and Acquisition Worldwide

Source: IMAA.(2018)

Table 2.4 Market Concentration, 1994–2010

	Year	Four-firm concentration ratio	Eight-firm concentration ratio
		Share of global market (percent)	
Crop seed and biotechnology	1994	21.1	29.0
	2000	32.5	43.1
	2009	53.9	63.4
Agricultural chemicals	1994	28.5	50.1
	2000	41.0	62.6
	2009	53.0	74.8
Farm machinery	1994	28.1	40.9
	2000	32.8	44.7
	2009	50.1	61.4
Animal health	1994	32.4	57.4
	2000	41.8	67.4
	2009	50.6	72.0
Animal genetics	1994	na	na
	2000	na	na
	2006/7	55.9	72.8

na= data not available. The concentration ratio measures the share of global market sales earned by the largest four of eight companies in the sector.
Source: USDA, Economic Research Service estimates from Fuglie et al. (2011)

plant genomics, chemical research, farm machinery, and consumer information. Figure 2.4 shows the increasing trend of mergers and acquisition, both in number and value, and that this trend reached a peak during the financial crisis of 2007–08. Looking just at the agricultural sector, we can see more than four hundred changes in property in the seed sector, starting from 1996 after the approval of the TRIPS Agreement (see Figure 2.5).

Two of the top ten seed companies are Chinese. ChemChina is the largest chemical firm in China, operating a wide range of businesses from basic chemicals to high-end manufacturing. In June 2018 ChemChina announced a merger with Sinochem, another large state-owned chemical conglomerate, which resulted in the world's largest industrial chemicals group, providing ChemChina with sufficient financial strength to absorb Syngenta.

Arrighi and Silver (1999: 121–23) describe a similar process that occurred during the Great Depression of 1873–96, in the shift from the U.K.

to the U.S. hegemonic cycle of capital accumulation, when existing enterprises had to organize among themselves in order to avoid the high level of
competitiveness in the market through horizontal and vertical integration:

> The Great Depression … marked the beginning of the transition
> from the British system of family business to the American system
> of vertically integrated, bureaucratically managed multinational
> corporations…. As Adam Smith had predicted a century earlier,
> the intensification of competitive pressures inherent in the process
> of trade liberalization had resulted in a curtailment of profits to
> a barely "tolerable" level…. One obvious means in this endeavor
> was horizontal combination—the fusion through association,
> merger, or takeover of enterprises using much the same inputs
> to make much the same outputs for much the same markets.…
> A more roundabout but, where feasible, more effective means of
> bringing the competition under control was vertical integration
> — the fusion, that is, of an enterprise's operations with those of
> its suppliers and customers, so as to ensure supplies "upstream"
> towards primary production, and outlets "downstream" towards

Figure 2.5 Number of Seed Industry Ownership Changes, 1996 to 2018

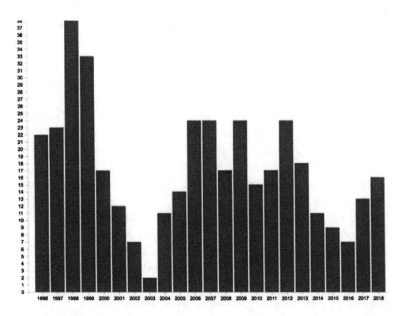

final consumption. The multi-unit enterprises that resulted from this fusion were in a position to reduce the transaction costs, risks, and uncertainties involved in moving inputs/outputs through the sequential subprocesses of production and exchange that linked the procurement of primary inputs to the disposal of final outputs.

This is relevant in order to find similarities between the same financial phases of the cycles of capital accumulation. Arrighi defines the financialization phase as a period of overcompetition and reorganization of the corporate structure in order to overcome the fall in profit rates and reestablish opportunities to invest in the real economy. In order to move from the financialization phase to a new material expansion, what is needed is an organizational revolution at the business level, which can shift capital accumulation from financial to material channels again.

Moore (2000, 2003, 2007, 2008, 2010c) elaborates on this aspect of Arrighi's theory, in which the organizational revolution of the production process during the financialization phase is the starting point for new material expansion. According to Moore's reading of Arrighi and world-systems theory, this shift from the financial to the material phase centres on agriculture. Indeed, each period of crisis emerges as the exhaustion of the organizational structures that created the new cycle of "material" accumulation and expansion. After a period of chaos and uncertainty, the cycle of accumulation comes to an end through the emergence of new business organizations, revolutionizing each state-capitalist relation and generating new opportunities for organizational revolutions of classes, states, and business organizations.

According to Moore (2011: 123), who has tried to explore a cyclically deepening relation between financialization and material life, "the financial circuit of capital and the commodity-centred transformation of human and extra-human natures are more tightly linked than Arrighi appears to suggest." Moore redefines the nature-capital categories at the core of the world-systems analysis, viewing the accumulation of capital as a socioecological process and reading capitalism as environmental history. In order to do that, he assumes two key concepts: the ecological surplus and the capitalization of nature. The ecological surplus stems from the combination of capitalized production (e.g., farm mechanization), and the appropriation of nature at zero cost (e.g., energy-intensive agriculture) is based on the appropriation of the geological production of nature (e.g., water and oil). In this sense, there is a dialectical unity between intensive capitalization and extensive appropriation. Moore (2010c: 395) traces the food surplus back to the

Figure 2.6 Timeline of Mergers and Acquisitions

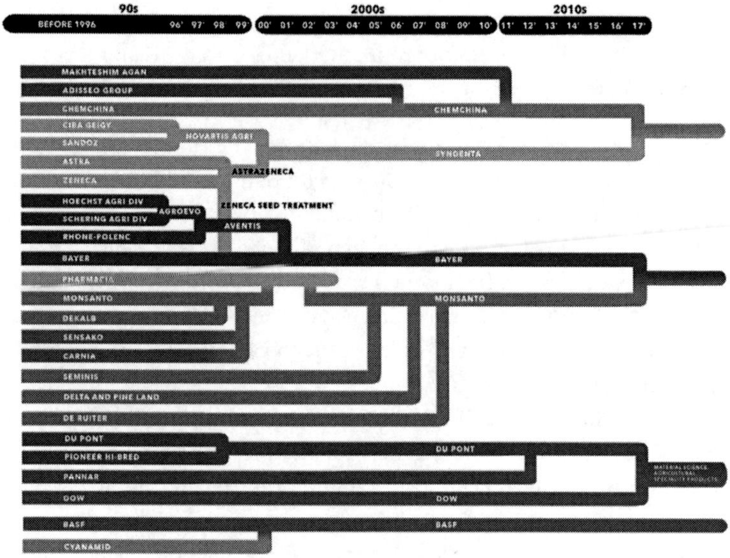

Source: African Center for Biodiversity (2017)

achievement of capitalist agricultural revolutions:

> For the greater part of six centuries, the relation between capital-
> ism and agriculture has been a remarkable one. In contrast with
> all previous civilizations, capitalism organized a series of extraor-
> dinary expansions of the food surplus, through successive agricul-
> tural revolutions. The "golden ages" of pre-capitalist civilizations
> invariably turned to the crisis so long as cultivation remained in
> the hands of peasants, who were not subject to market discipline.
> Sooner or later demographic expansion undercut land and labour
> productivity, and along with it, the agricultural surplus available
> for commercial and manufacturing growth in the broader social
> economy. Such had been the case with feudalism.

It is important to highlight that the capitalist system started with the
subjection of peasants to market discipline. Moore (2010c: 395–96) states
that agriculture plays a foundational role in the capitalist system, identifying
the cheapness of food as the main driver that defines the cost of reproduction for the whole economic system — cheaper food means lower wages
and increasing profits:

Capitalism achieved its long-run economic expansion by means of imposing bourgeois property relations in the countryside, compelling the transition from peasant producer to capitalist farmer. With the transition to capitalism, the imposition of private property in land, backed by the power of the modern state (and its imperial formations), propelled a process of dispossession and differentiation that enabled rising labour productivity in agriculture and a rising food surplus. Vast reservoirs of labour power took shape to feed the satanic mills, and vast agricultural surpluses were mobilized to feed these workers. From the Dutch and English agricultural revolutions of the early modern era to the family farm and Green Revolutions of the nineteenth and twentieth centuries, the bloody expropriations of capital have justified themselves on the basis of this signal achievement ("modernization").

The road to the modern world, it seems, has been paved with cheap food. As noted earlier, food, energy and inputs are "cheap" to the degree that they are produced, and otherwise mobilized, at significantly lower costs than the systemwide average, and at significantly high volumes to *drive down* the costs of production for the system as a whole. The price of food is so pivotal because it conditions the price of labour. The great eras of capitalist development have always been conditioned on massive demographic expansion *and* massive proletarianization. The signal contribution of agricultural revolutions to the course of capitalist development can be found here, in driving down the relative cost of food while driving forward proletarianization.

Cheap food influences the price of labour, which determines the production costs for the system as a whole. Historically, the development of capitalism was rooted in demographic expansion, thus increasing the process of proletarianization. In this sense, Moore clarifies that the food-labour relationship is the core relationship of capitalist development, since the price of food determines the value of commodified labour power and the capacity of capital to extract surplus value.

All of the Arrighian hegemonic cycles of accumulation in Moore are therefore based on organizational revolutions in agriculture. In the British period, too, capitalist accumulation developed along two frontiers: a vertical one, for coal extraction *into* the Earth, and a horizontal one, for producing commodities *across* the Earth. Adapting Arrighi's (1994) language, Moore

(2010c: 391) affirms that we are facing the *crisis* of an ecological regime when the conditions for an expansion of the ecological surplus start to erode and "food, energy and inputs become more, rather than less, expensive." Ecological regimes ensure adequate flows of energy, food, raw materials, and labour surpluses to the centre of the worldwide system of accumulation. Markets and institutions organize nature, and the decisive divide is between the town (consuming surplus) and countryside (producing surplus).

> All great waves of capital accumulation have unfolded through a greatly expanded ecological surplus, manifested in cheap food, cheap energy and cheap inputs. The creation of this ecological surplus is central to accumulation over the *longue durée*. There is a dialectic between capital's capacity to appropriate biophysical and social natures at low cost, and its immanent tendency to capitalize the reproduction of labour power and extra-human natures....

> Marx's theory of underproduction crisis — he calls it a "general law" of accumulation — argues that "the rate of profit is inversely proportional to the value of the raw materials".... There is an important tension between the "overproduction of machinery," and the "underproduction" of raw materials. (Moore, 2010c: 392–93)

Many similarities can be found between Moore's approach and David Harvey's (2003) chapter on accumulation by dispossession. For instance, Harvey (2003: 139) writes, "It is also possible to accumulate in the face of stagnant effective demand if the costs of inputs (land, raw materials, intermediate inputs, labour power) decline significantly. Access to cheaper inputs is, therefore, just as important as access to widening markets in keeping profitable opportunities open." The contradiction in historical capitalism has been to preserve and create — while simultaneously undermining and appropriating — the ecologies that reproduce autonomously from the circuit of capital: the "rising capitalization of nature creates a world-historical situation of rising production costs stemming from the degradation of the conditions of production" (Moore 2010c: 405). Therefore, rising socio-ecological exhaustion and the rising capitalization of nature are two sides of the same coin.

Moore explains that the Green Revolution was characterized by an incredible expansion of relative ecological surplus, constituting a new phase in the capitalization of global nature — both nonhuman (cheap grains and energy) and human (relative surplus population expanding the reserve army of labour through mechanization and labour intensification, and through the class differentiation of peasants) — that created the conditions for the lowest food market prices in the world's history. While capitalism massively expanded the relative ecological surplus (cheap food, energy, and materials) through an imperialist policy of new resource appropriation, it also tried to intensify its penetration into the marginal zones of undercapitalized nature.

Concurrently, the Green Revolution experienced different problems: a trend toward farm concentration and energy inefficiency, with a rise in energy prices, along with an erosion of the capacity to govern biophysical natures, which in turn escalated the resource depletion of water and soil and the superweed effect. In the age of the Green Revolution, the two contradictions of agriculture came into play, gradually wearing down the mechanisms that could be used to deliver (or even sustain) an ecological surplus that was sufficient to expand accumulation. The opportunities and obstacles of the political ecology of nature as capital circulate through (and not merely around) biophysical circuits: the faster these ecological revolutions are, the more they function toward the imprisonment — rather than liberation — of accumulation. Moore (2010c: 409) concludes that "the relative ecological surplus falls as the capitalization of global nature proceeds."

This theoretical framework proposed by Moore, based on the historical analysis of capitalist development, allows us to question whether the present neoliberal phase of financialization represents the final moment of a structural crisis of capitalism or whether it is just a phase that can be resolved through new conditions of accumulation. If an ecological surplus characterizes every phase of capitalism, where today can such surpluses be found and produced? Is the neoliberal world order bringing the world system toward an "agricultural revolution in reverse" (Braudel 1972: 427), with a constant decline in labour productivity and the relative food surplus?

Moore (2010c) states that neoliberalism in agriculture has been characterized by the Uruguay Round of multilateral trade negotiations in 1986 and the Marrakesh Agreement of 1994 (which resulted in the establishment of the WTO), leading to the decoupling of world market prices from production costs (McMichael 2005) and therefore to two major consequences. The first is a decrease in world food prices; according to FAO data, "world food prices dropped by 39 per cent between 1975 and 1989, and still further in the decade that followed" (Moore 2010c: 278), a trend that continued up until the world food crisis in 2007–08. The second is the concentration and centralization of capital in the agri-food sector (see Figures 2.3 and 2.4, and Table 2.4).

Indeed, in Moore's analysis, neoliberalism as a historical phase of the current cycle of capital accumulation has not generated the conditions for new growth and real social development: we did not witness a "third technological revolution" allowing for an organizational shift that could lift up profits and start a new material expansion of the economy. According to Moore (2010c: 390), the failure of GMO crops represents the neoliberal failure in transforming agriculture: "Nearly three decades of experimentation with genetically modified organisms has succeeded in transferring wealth and power from farmers to big capital without any success in raising intrinsic yields."

How does financialization of agriculture fit into this analysis? Moore enlarges Arrighi's approach by introducing the great frontier concept as a premise for the appropriation of natural resources and a deeper understanding of the Marxian metabolic rift. The frontier may be external or internal to capital circuits — external for uncommodified nature or internal for existing circuits by eliminating "inefficiencies" and restructuring production. Moore (2010c: 402) writes:

> The transition from "old" to "new" agrarian questions during the 1970s, suggested for very different reasons by Bernstein (2001) and McMichael (1997), points to the exhaustion of capitalism's agro-ecological frontiers, set in motion during the long sixteenth century. While there are still forests and tracts of "underutilized" land to enclose and exploit, today's frontiers are but drops in the bucket relative to the demands of value accumulation. Frontiers are not merely places "out there" (and out of time) but are constituted by the varying logics of systemic reproduction in its successive developmental phases. This closure of the "Great Frontier" (Webb 1964) marks an epochal transition in the history of capitalism. The closure of resource, labour and waste frontiers has cut off a key avenue of capital's escape from the rising costs of production.

> The rising capitalization of world agriculture — through which the farm becomes the agro-ecological pivot of "downstream" and "upstream" commodification — not only amplifies the tendency towards a declining rate of profit but in equal measure amplifies the pressures to escape it, through efforts to extend the frontier of "technical control."

The crucial theoretical passage is the introduction of the Marxian dialectic between underproduction (too few inputs) and overproduction (too many commodities); according to this vision, the current crisis emerges as an insufficient flow of cheap food, fuel, labour, and energy to the productive circuit of capital (M-C-M′). The neoliberal crisis has to do with the incapacity to produce the relative ecological surplus that previous cycles of accumulation produced through an agricultural revolution that generated a great leap in yields (shift of the external frontier with a small capital investment), rather than a simple increase based on a better allocation of resources (internal frontier).

In Moore's view, in order to start a new era of cheap food, neoliberalism has relied on the biotechnological revolution and the wave of new "enclosures." Even if this process supports the redistribution of income, deepening the class differentiation process among farmers and the proletarianization process, it has not delivered any real growth in yields, or at least not enough to create a new expansion of production within a new systemic cycle of accumulation. According to Moore, the new GMO varieties are at the core of a new yield revolution but are not delivering the expected leap in food production with small capital investment. (In reality, the aim of the globalization of agricultural biotechnology was not to increase yields, but to stop the progressive decline in yield growth worldwide. In this case too, the failure was clear, as superweeds have evolved to survive herbicides, which the example of Roundup Ready crops demonstrates [Benbrook 2012]. The result was a quicker evolution of biophysical nature than what capital can control.) The Union of Concerned Scientists (2009: 3–4), in *Failure to Yield: Biotechnology's Broken Promises*, concludes that "most yield gains are attributable to non-genetic engineering approaches" and "GE [genetic engineering] technology has produced neither intrinsic nor operational yield gains in commercialized varieties."

Moore (2010c: 400) considers the superweed effect to be an explanatory phenomenon related to the biotech field's failure to deliver a new agricultural revolution and a new cycle of accumulation based on commercial expansion:

This "*superweed effect*" marks one aspect of agriculture's *differentia specifica* in Marx's important — if too often neglected — argument, noted earlier, that the "overproduction" of machinery (fixed capital) tends towards the "underproduction" of raw materials (circulating capital). Rising costs of energy and inputs used in a given production cycle reinforce the tendency towards a declining rate of profit inscribed in rising mechanization. As capital invested in machinery overtakes that spent on wages, therefore, the very productivity gains achieved by mechanization and standardization set in motion widening demands for circulating capital (inputs).

But the production of energy, wood, metals, fibres and other inputs is rooted in socio-ecological processes that do not respond quickly or easily to market signals.

Using Marx's theory of value, Moore defines the overproduction of machinery as the consequence of the underproduction of raw materials. This means that in the neoliberal age, agriculture should find a way to increase labour productivity. To do so, the new strategy is to discipline and organize this increase in productivity by intervening in biophysical nature at a cellular and even genetic level, therefore extending the area for commodity production and exchange to include in the capitalist cycle of accumulation that part of nature that is not yet subsumed by capital. Moore assumes that in the neoliberal phase, the opportunities for capital to appropriate nature (through the expansion of the external frontier) are reduced. The superweed effect exemplifies how biotech cannot maintain the yields of the Green Revolution.

The closure of the great frontier (Webb 1964) leaves a small margin for a better allocation of underutilized resources (deepening of the internal frontier), as these are not able to restart the capital accumulation process and avoid the rising costs of production. Moore underlines how the previous drivers of agricultural revolutions were based on different forms of bourgeois territorial and property relations, technical innovations, and still available uncapitalized or undercapitalized nature. After the end of Bretton Woods and during the neoliberal financial expansion, there was an increase in property claims on the genetic diversity of the biosphere. Even if Moore (2010c: 406) suspends his judgement on whether the biotech revolution could provide a way forward, he notices how the financialization of the neoliberal era has marked the transition from "the 'formal' to the 'real subsumption of nature to capital.'" He disagrees with the vision of Neil Smith (2007: 33), who describes GMOs as creating the conditions for a new phase of accumulation characterized by capitalization "all the way down" to the genetic relations of life itself. "A new frontier in the production of nature has rapidly opened up, namely a *vertical integration of nature* into capital," writes Smith. "This involves not just the production of nature 'all the way down,' but its simultaneous financialization 'all the way up.' Capital is no longer content simply to plunder an available nature but rather increasingly moves to produce an inherently social nature as the basis of new sectors of production and accumulation."

Moore's analysis, based on Arrighi's and Krippner's definition of financialization, allows us to interpret the data on mergers and acquisitions not as a verification of Clapp and Isakson's shareholder value hypothesis, but as a demonstration of the fall in profit rates and the tendency toward concentration of enterprises to gather enough resources in research and development to develop an organizational revolution. While the visions of Moore on the one side, and Clapp and Isakson on the other side, coincide on the characterization of financialization through new financial arenas for investment, Clapp and Isakson's understanding of financialization as shareholder value is less explanatory than Moore's organizational revolutions, which implicitly assume a definition of financialization not based on the nature of the actors involved but on the phase of the cycle of accumulation.

Moore's conceptualization of capitalism as a world ecology is relevant to better defining the role of agriculture in Arrighi's analysis regarding hegemonic cycles of capital accumulation and to connecting this analysis with the broader analysis of the financialization of nature. First, in his analysis of agriculture, Arrighi (2007) noticed how the surplus capital accumulated in cities brought into existence in contiguous rural areas commercial agriculture oriented toward the production of food for the urban population, penetrating rural structures and deepening the process of proletarianization of the peasantry. He also recalled the Smithian distinction between the *natural progress* of China and the *unnatural progress* of European nations, the former being directed toward the agricultural sector first, then manufacturing, and finally foreign trade, whereas the latter started with foreign trade, then developed manufacturing and agriculture. According to this scheme, the capital invested in agriculture was more stable and secure. Moore shows how the overaccumulation of capital during financialization flows to the countryside to find *new financial arenas*: by reshaping agriculture and investing in an organizational revolution of the production system, the financialization phase shifts back to material expansion. A good example of this trend is found in Fairbairn's (2014: 779) analysis, where the overaccumulation of capital reaches the farmland with the objective of portfolio differentiation, but at the same time does not prevent the reorganization of production: "Land plays two different economic roles; it is an essential factor of production, but it also acts as a reserve of value and creates wealth through passive appreciation. In other words, it is a productive asset that moonlights as a financial asset."

A second way that Moore's idea of capitalism as a world ecology is relevant to Arrighi's analysis is that it allows for connecting to another approach to financialization: the so-called financialization of nature, as defined by Friends of the Earth International (2015). In order to efficiently allocate natural resources and ecosystem services, new markets are generated with titles to be exchanged (in order to efficiently allocate resources through the market) or payment schemes.

> The UNEP [United Nations Environment Programme], the World Business Council for Sustainable Development, the World Bank and others promoting a Green Economy say that "green growth" will address these multiple crises in one sweep. Green growth, they claim, will relieve states of the growing financial burden of environmental protection while fixing the environmental damage corporate destruction of nature has already caused.

> "Green growth," however, redefines "green" not "growth": Nature is described in the language of financial capital to better suit the new Green Economy. This Green Economy needs a flexible idea of nature. A nature divided into different "ecosystem services" that can be quantified, measured and above all, broken up into individual units, so profit can be made from selling rights to these individual units of nature. We call this financialization of nature. (Friends of the Earth International 2015: 2)

Therefore, natural resources, or any other underlying asset, must be efficiently allocated according to a neoclassical approach, thus creating a new market of titles virtually representing the underlying assets.

Researchers of environmental economics claim that the pricing of nature will promote the environmental sustainability of the markets, leading to a new green economy:

> The green economy, therefore, constitutes a new capitalist strategy involving the redirecting of investments towards nature, which is transformed into "natural capital," with markets created and prices established around it. Pollution and conservation serve as the basis for new business activities; new supposedly "clean" technologies like agrofuels are promoted, but implemented under the same intensive, large-scale model that implies more land grabbing and social and environmental impacts; new markets are created around nature, such as the "carbon emissions market," which forms part of the financial markets; and a leading role is given to corporations.

> Thus financialization forms part of the green economy and complements it perfectly, because both concepts aim in the same direction: commodification and speculation around all aspects of

life. It is an intolerable approach for those of us who are struggling to stop the destruction of forests and other important natural areas around the world, which do not have a price, but do have enormous value for local communities and humanity as a whole. (World Rainforest Movement 2012)

It is interesting to observe how financialization and the green economy are understood as sharing the aim of commodifying and speculating on all aspects of life. The relationship between financialization and commodification seems to be a circular one. In this sense, it is enlightening to start with the definition of financialization of agriculture developed by Luigi Russi (2014: 93–94):

> The expansionism of the economic system under the pressure of the financial system increasingly translates into the dismembering of organic cycles of production, as embodied in peasant co-production, into linear input-output chains subject to the metric of financial profit. Farm production is increasingly dependent on external inputs (e.g. chemical fertilizers, pesticides, hybrid or genetically modified seeds, mechanical implements such as tractors) and on external output markets for agricultural commodities. When it is not outright displaced by the re-articulation of land into new assemblages which may or may not serve to produce food (e.g., biofuel production in the "land grab"). In this new environment, transnational corporations both in the processing and the retail sector increasingly have the ability to exert control over the food chain, and enact new orderings that are streamlined for the extraction of financial value.

Russi describes financialization as dismantling and linearizing the complex relations of coproduction between man and nature embodied in the food system, which are swallowed up by an expanding economic system. In reality, the process of a linear transformation of the model of production in an input-output chain is no different from the commodification process that has been put in place already by the Green Revolution and industrial agriculture. Van der Ploeg (2010: 1) writes, "Harriet Friedmann (1980: 158) defined commoditization as the 'penetration into reproduction of commodity relations.' Accordingly, 'commoditization is a process of deepening commodity relations within the cycle of reproduction. Commoditization occurs to the extent that each household … comes to depend increasingly on commodity relations for reproduction.'" The commodification of agriculture, therefore, serves as a precondition for financial products (e.g., derivatives), since it preceded the financialization process itself.

The incomplete transition to capitalism in agriculture is a precondition for the financialization of agriculture, as assumed by Moore with the great frontier closure. In the context of the closure of the great frontier, it is important to keep a clear distinction between the commodification process (related to the commercial expansion phase of the capitalist cycles of accumulation) and the financialization phase: commodification is still oriented toward the generation of profits through the production process, whereas financialization is not. Having clarified the distinction and the relation between commodification and financialization, the confusion stems from the fact that as financialization penetrates the countryside, it polarizes and proletarianizes rural areas.

If we apply the Arrighian approach of Moore to the green economy and view it as the creation of new markets for capital investments, we should assume that carbon credits and carbon finance are not part of the financialization of agriculture, since they are not oriented toward an organizational revolution, even if they are part of the financial capital flow toward new financial arenas:

> Nature's appeal to capital markets and corporations differs in this latest redefinition because they are not primarily interested in creating a new physical commodity from nature. There will be no value extraction through a physical good. No visible product will be extracted, transported, processed and sold. In the case of ecosystem services, the value lies in the potential to reduce corporate compliance costs arising from environmental legislation and to enable continuing industrial production despite increasing global limits on "resource use." The economic value lies in a market that offers permission to destroy or pollute nature in places that are of interest to capital markets and corporations but where legal or moral restrictions limit the destruction. Ecosystem service markets offer this permission in the form of offset credits. (Friends of the Earth International 2015: 6)

In this case too, we can use the term "financialization" to capture *capital free of its commodity form*. As mentioned above, in Arrighi's and Moore's work the overaccumulation of capital leads to the overflow of capital in the countryside, which is intended to be one of the many new financial arenas (Clapp and Isakson 2018a), equal to flex crops (Borras et al. 2012), real estate, and nature in general. The financialization process, therefore, creates new markets, with tradable stocks of an underlying asset (e.g., carbon emissions) absorbing a relevant part of the financial capital. As with the carbon market, the case of financial derivatives of commodities is crystal clear. In the capital flow across different financial arenas, and due to falling profits and merger and acquisition processes, increasing interstate and interbusiness competition for financial resources creates a push toward new organizational processes, which in agriculture allow for decreasing the costs of reproduction and labour for the worldwide system while increasing margins and reestablishing profitability. This distinction is relevant to understanding the significance of the financialization process as a whole and its specific role in agriculture.

Ghosh (2011) is correct in assuming that the food price crisis cannot be treated as a separate issue from the global financial crisis. Even McMichael (2012) reads the current penetration of international capital markets in agriculture, including land-grabbing, as ultimately undermining the conditions that allow capital to reproduce. The capitalization of nonhuman nature corresponds to what Moore calls the underreproduction of nature. In this phenomenon, capital takes precedence over the natural world and exhausts ecosystems, progressively expanding and penetrating new frontiers of accumulation that serve as temporary solutions to the accumulation crisis. McMichael identifies the framework for this further penetration in the World Bank's 2008 *World Development Report* on "agriculture for development," where the crisis was tackled through further inclusion of small-scale food producers in global value chains, transforming the low-yield model of peasant production into a highly capitalized productive model with intense use of natural resources. According to McMichael, land and water enclosure is the premise for a new extractive paradigm that is centred on biomass and synthetic biology and that legally appropriates living systems through technology and patents and titles.

Harvey (2003: 139) discusses how "new mechanisms of accumulation by dispossession" undervalue raw materials. In the specific case of agriculture, the TRIPS Agreement undervalues the peasant seed systems through intellectual property rights: "The patenting and licensing of genetic material, seed plasma, and all manner of other products can now be used against whole populations whose practices had played a crucial role in the development of those materials" (Harvey 2003: 151). Further, "the analogy with the creation of an industrial reserve army by throwing people out of work is exact. Valuable assets are thrown out of circulation and devalued. They lie fallow and dormant until surplus capital seizes upon them to breathe new life into capital accumulation.... The umbilical cord that ties together accumulation by dispossession and expanded reproduction is that given by finance capital and the institutions of credit, backed, as ever, by state powers" (Harvey 2003: 139–52). Finance is intended as money capital that creates a new market of underlying assets outside of the accumulation regime. It does not increase profits through growth in productivity or material expansion of trade, but through capital gains that appropriate *raw materials* outside of the capitalist market. In the specific case of agriculture, some inputs are crucial to production.

In the Arrighi-Moore paradigm, the capitalist accumulation regime finds its funding premise in the capital penetration of the countryside: it increases yields and lowers the cost of raw materials (agricultural inputs) to reduce food costs, lower wages, and increase profits. If the capital penetration of the countryside does not generate agricultural innovation, the accumulation regime will shift to a financialization phase in order to maintain profits and then revert back to the countryside as an *agrifinancialization* process, which operates through accumulation by dispossession and intensifies the proletarianization and class differentiation of peasantry that still persists in the fields through the model of peasant agriculture. This process involves the dispossession of collective rights and forms of property (such as seeds), ultimately increasing accumulation.

It is worth noting how Harvey (2003: 149–50) describes the mechanism of financialization, assuming the framework of austerity policies:

> What accumulation by dispossession does is to release a set of assets (including labour power) at very low (and in some instances zero) cost. Over-accumulated capital can seize hold of such assets and immediately turn them to profitable use.... Another way would be to release cheap raw materials (such as oil) into the system....
>
> The same goal can be achieved, however, by the devaluation of existing capital assets and labour power. Devalued capital assets can be bought up at fire-sale prices and profitably recycled back into the circulation of capital by overaccumulated capital. But this requires a prior wave of devaluation, which means a crisis of some kind. Crises may be orchestrated, managed, and controlled to rationalize the system. This is often what state-administered austerity programmes, making use of the key levers of interest rates and the credit system, are often all about. Limited crises may

be imposed by external force upon one sector or upon a territory or whole territorial complex of capitalist activity. This is what the international financial system (led by the IMF) backed by superior state power (such as that of the United States) is so expert at doing. The result is the periodic creation of a stock of devalued, and in many instances undervalued, assets in some part of the world, which can be put to profitable use by the capital surpluses that lack opportunities elsewhere.

In this case, austerity policies and financial crises devalue and grab resources through accumulation by dispossession. This financial mechanism functions thanks to the crisis and devaluation of assets and aims to transfer property. Harvey, therefore, contributes to understanding how financialization functions through accumulation by dispossession: the lack of protection of a collective resource or right (i.e., a raw material that is crucial to defining the cost of food production) allows for its dispossession and integration into the capitalist production system, ultimately fostering a new material expansion. The next chapters discuss which raw materials that agrifinancialization is devaluing and investing in, within the context of the closure of the agroecological frontier, as described by Moore. He sees GMOs as the failure of such an attempt to integrate biodiversity into capitalist production, due to the superweed effect and the lack of ability to increase the yields of agricultural production. It is also worth noting the common definition of financialization as an abstraction of food, which has similarities to the definition of financialization as an abstraction of capital from the commodity form into M-M′. Moore (2010a) mentions the concept, explaining the deepening of the abstraction of food through its conversion to fuel.

So financialization has nothing to do with the distinction regarding whether investors are part of the financial sector or the commercial one: what makes the difference is the form in which capital is invested in order to reproduce itself and generate profits. For instance, if we identify the financial sector with banks, could the fact that banks are investing in companies rather than providing credit be seen as a financial investment in which capital is not assuming the commodity form? This is not the case. Even if the capital investment is directed to the control of the company, the capital is still part of the circulating capital of the company and can therefore feed the productive cycle of the company.

What about the case in which control of a company's capital majority leads to a merger with other companies? The mergers and acquisitions process could be a symptom of a fall in profit (which is typical of the financialization phase in Arrighi's analysis) and the reorganization of production. However, according to Arrighi, the mergers and acquisitions process on a vast scale is not financialization per se. It is just a context in which financialization happens, in which capital does not find any remuneration and will search for it through a reorganization of production, so as to reduce the costs of production and reinforce the monopolistic position, or through a direct investment in a financial asset on a short-term basis. For instance, if an investment in the shares of a company were to lead to mergers and acquisitions that could increase the share value of the company, and the shares were then sold in the short term on the market, that would be a financial investment that could be described as financialization and financial speculation at the same time. However, this is not the case. First, mergers and acquisitions lead to a concentration of the sector, and there is no evidence of the dismissal of shares on the market afterwards or the spin-off of part of a company (as happened on a vast scale in the 1980s). Second, it would be questionable to define this speculative movement as M-M′, since the capital investment would be illiquid and immobilized in a productive system for a while.

This is not the case of financial derivatives of commodities, which are assimilated to cash, being totally liquid. The case of financial derivatives of agricultural commodities goes in this direction: agricultural commodities are used as collateral (a real product to be consumed) for financial exchanges in futures markets. Due to the deregulation of financial markets, the quantity of commodities exchanged there is higher than the real quantity produced in the world. Therefore, financial speculation does not provide liquidity to the commodity market but instead defines and disturbs the prices of agricultural commodities for the benefit of financial interests. Commodity prices are driven by financial speculation trends and not the real underlying production. Agricultural production (including stocks and food reserves) is a secondary aspect driven by financial speculation. The case of financial derivatives clearly shows how finance uses an underlying asset (the collateral) to create a financial market and generate profits and capital gains through speculation, in the broader framework of the deregulation of financial markets. This was the case during the world food price crisis of 2006–08 (and later again in 2011), when food prices witnessed a period of extraordinary volatility, peaking (by several hundred per cent) at the end of 2007 and in the first half of 2008.

During the twentieth century, the correlation between agricultural commodity prices and the price of oil was 0.07, whereas the correlation between the price of oil and commodity average prices was 0.23 (Newell 2008). After the adoption of the U.S. Energy Policy Act in 2005, and with the subsequent introduction of a futures contract on ethanol at the Chicago Board of Trade and the large-scale adoption of new ethanol-based agrofuels by the U.S. transport sector, the correlation between agricultural commodity prices and the price of oil increased to 0.93. When the ethanol futures contracts were introduced, over-the-counter derivatives were exempted from any regulation designed to limit the ability of market participants to manipulate the market (i.e., position limits), as outlined in the U.S. Commodity Futures Modernization Act of 2000.

Commodity index funds enabled investors to benefit from different commodity futures markets without having to invest directly in each single commodity future. Given that commodity futures markets are predominantly traded over-the-counter, they entail customized bilateral contracts made directly between two contracting parties and lack the transparency of trades on an open exchange at the stock market. With commodity index funds, speculators were not interested in buying underlying goods or in short-term movements in futures prices. Their strategy was to "go long": to continually buy back futures contracts purchased at a lower price and resell them at a higher price before their deadline, thus reinvesting in futures with a later maturity. Financial analysts fed this process by providing forecasts of further price increases. Real market players were encouraged to increase their agricultural reserves in anticipation of future earnings, thus increasing farm prices by reducing supply in accordance with the traditional speculative approach (Conti 2012; Ghosh 2010; High Level Panel of Experts on Food Security and Nutrition 2011; Krippner, Lemoine, and Ravelli 2018; Sivini 2009). Figure 2.7 shows the rising volume of investments in commodity index funds since 2004, after the implosion of the housing market (Ghosh 2010) and the U.S. Energy Policy Act.

The correlation between oil and agricultural products prices comes from a process that attributes a price to an asset independent of the real economy and underlying economic fundamentals such as supply and demand. Indeed, the analysis of the price and cost relation refers to two different channels of transmission: the first one is financial, while the second is embedded in the production system and in supply chains. This makes clear the division between a financial determination of prices and a determination of costs based on the real economy. An independent estimate (Epstein 2008) calculated that for soybeans, speculative positions bought 59.1 percent of the 2007 U.S. domestic crop, while for wheat the figures were higher, reaching 83.6 percent. Thus, the changes in food prices did not reflect movements in

Figure 2.7 Commodity Index Investments Trends

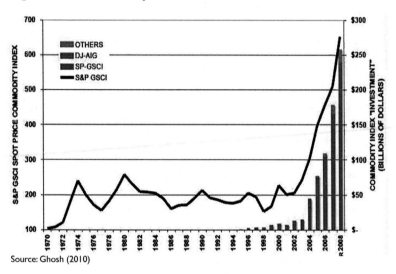

Source: Ghosh (2010)

market supply or demand. The main driver was the speculative deals: these not only provided liquidity to the market, they also drove it.

Although agrofuels have a role in the current food crisis, blaming price volatility on agrofuel demand shocks was misleading. Supply or demand shocks cannot explain price volatility, which corresponds to a series of price changes heading in opposite directions and is neither predictable nor explainable through supply and demand fundamentals. Agricultural production has been in a state of constant growth since 1960, and when the food crisis erupted in 2007 the food supply system was more than capable of meeting the demand of the current world population (FAO 2011). Analyses based on supply and demand shocks erroneously assume that food price volatility relies on real processes (e.g., substitution effect on supply and demand of agrofuels and agricultural commodities) (Conti 2012).

Meanwhile, farmers in developing countries responded to rising food prices by investing and borrowing to expand their production — thus exposing themselves to the risk of being wiped out as global food prices dropped. This phenomenon led to bankruptcy and the abandonment of production by small farmers. Financial speculation in agricultural commodities, and the subsequent food price volatility, helped the concentration of agribusiness evict the weaker actors from the market and created the conditions through which agribusiness could increase its profits by transferring price management from the futures market to the real market, as the latter could be kept under full control. Agri-food businesses shifted more toward financial markets and gained an increasing share of returns from financial activities, while financial actors influenced the price and control of farmland and the formation of food prices.

Coming back to Arrighi and Moore, the financialization of agriculture is the consequence of a fall in profits: there is disinvestment from real agricultural production and a shift toward financial deals. Overaccumulation and underproduction explains through the fall in profitability both the mergers and acquisitions driving the concentration of agribusiness (aiming to increase profitability through the monopolist control of the market, rather than the minor effect of cost saving) and the financialization of agriculture. Mergers and acquisitions are therefore still part of the final phase of commercial expansion of the capital accumulation cycle. In the particular case of agriculture, financialization relies on the process of commodification that agribusiness generated through capital penetration into the countryside (from this we derive the term "agrifinancialization," which highlights the consequentiality and unity of the historical processes of accumulation in agriculture). The streamlining of the complexity of food systems into an input-output process, as Russi (2014) explained clearly, through the Green Revolution was the precondition for the financialization process, even if this was separated from financialization itself.

The question therefore is, what is the financialization of agriculture and how does it work? Assuming the definition of financialization as money capital that "sets itself free from its commodity form," the financialization of agriculture is the abstraction of food from its physical form, fostering capital accumulation through financial deals. The result is derivatives of agricultural commodities as pure money capital that has been liberated from its commodity form through financial abstraction. At the same time, agrifinancialization works to produce organizational innovation in agriculture so as to trigger a new phase of material expansion, working along the internal and external frontiers of capital accumulation. GMOs and synthetic biology are clearly identified by Moore, Smith, Harvey, and McMichael as the new frontiers. Moore assumes that the superweed effect marks the end of GMOs as the innovation was meant to restart capital accumulation. Smith sees GMOs as the vertical integration of nature into capital. Harvey considers them the target of accumulation by dispossession as perpetrated by the WTO and TRIPS agreements, and McMichael considers GMOs as the base of the new bioeconomy approach that is transforming the hydrocarbons industry. This rich theoretical discussion sets the stage for the next chapter, which looks at the ongoing negotiations and processes in the FAO and the United Nations.

3 Transnational Governance of Agriculture

The financialization process generated by the end of the Bretton Woods agreements resulted in neoliberal globalization. As the role of nation-states has waned, the IMF, the World Bank, the United Nations, and other global governance institutions have played a key part in mainstreaming neoliberal policies in agriculture.

Until the end of the Bretton Woods agreements, the GATT was the main instrument of support for the formation of a world market under the jurisdiction of the U.S. government, which controlled the pace and direction of the liberalization of trade. The final outcome was not a free trade system, but a patchwork of agreements between the United States, Japan, Europe, and other minor countries. Since the end of Bretton Woods, U.S. policies have been supported by the IMF, the World Bank, and the United Nations.

Indeed, the Bretton Woods agreements were established after World War II, when the hegemony of the United States (Arrighi 1994; Arrighi and Silver 1999) in global markets was based on a process of "internalization" of the world market within giant domestic business organizations, leaving U.S. economic activities organically integrated into a single national reality to a greater extent than they ever were during the British cycle. In this context, foreign direct investment by U.S. TNCs transferred managerial control over substantial sectors of foreign economies to U.S. nationals. TNCs have integrated the production and distribution process into a single flow, from the sourcing of inputs to the disposal of final outputs, succeeding in subordinating business risk and uncertainties along the value chain to long-term business planning (Arrighi 1994, 2007).

In addition, until the 1970s, the U.S. Federal Reserve System had effective control over the world's liquidity and was able to promote and sustain a generalized expansion of world trade in a way that has few precedents in capitalist history, playing a major role compared to the IMF and the

World Bank in the regulation of the world's money. It was only with the crisis of U.S. hegemony in the 1970s and, above all, in the 1980s that for the first time the Bretton Woods organizations, such as the IMF and the World Bank, rose to prominence in global monetary regulation. By the time Bretton Woods ended, TNCs were embedded in a world-scale system of production, exchange, and accumulation that was independent of any state authority and ruled the members of the interstate system, including the United States.

TNCs played a role in the accumulation of surplus capital in European and offshore markets that led to a crisis of the central banks' regulation of money supply in accordance with the Bretton Woods regime. The phase of financial expansion began in 1968 with the explosive growth of TNC deposits in the London-centred Eurodollar market, forcing the U.S. government to abandon the gold-dollar exchange standard and hand over to the free forces of the market the ability to fix the prices of national currencies. The United States tried to support material expansion through its monetary policies, but the expansive policies fuelled the petrodollar and Eurodollar deposits through the private interbank mechanism of the money supply. The end of Bretton Woods saw the beginning of a new neoliberal economic framework of austerity, economic structural adjustment programs, and bilateral and multilateral trade agreements led by the World Bank and IMF — such as the Uruguay Round of GATT negotiations that culminated in the formation of the WTO in 1995:

> From the 1980s onward, nation-states have been squeezed three ways by neoliberalism: (1) "from below" through a widespread push for political and fiscal decentralization and administrative de-concentration; (2) "from the side" through far-reaching privatization of governance structures and responsibilities; and (3) "from above" through globalization and the partial giving up of significant state powers to international inter-governmental and financial institutions. (Borras 2016: 13)

This process created a new space for what is called global governance, with the triple squeeze of national state regulatory powers, or *nonterritorial governance* (Coleman and Wayland 2006), which transcends the concept of a territory created by nation-states and focuses on the relationships between social actors, nation-states, and international organizations. In this sense, governance can be seen as a series of different sites of policy decision-making that may lack coherence: the agreed actions and political outcomes emerging in two different places may not be coordinated and may contradict each other.

The triple squeeze of national state powers corresponds to fragmentation and an unordered political space, characterized by a mixture of formal and informal structures and the penetrability of hierarchies:

> Borders and boundaries for policymaking are variable and porous and are being created and re-created in response to globalizing processes and policy developments. In transnational spaces, states "act" alongside a range of nonstate actors. In these spaces, however, the symmetry and congruence between decisionmakers and citizens characteristic of "territorial governance" is lost. Some analysts suggest that global civil society can help address this loss by creating direct linkages between global policymaking and citizens. (Coleman and Wayland 2006: 246)

Until the 1970s, agricultural policies were discussed by the different ministries, and the global organizations were not involved. Not even the developed countries attended OECD meetings. As a result, relationships at the transnational level were practically episodic. In order to leave the power of decision-making at the domestic market level, the GATT had established some exceptions for health and safety and for agricultural trade, such as quantitative restrictions on imports of agricultural goods, to control domestic supply and export subsidies on primary products.

The Uruguay Round Agreement on Agriculture replaced nontariff barriers with bound tariff rates (i.e., most-favoured-nation tariff rate, incorporated as an integral component of a country's schedule of concessions or commitments to other WTO members). Further, export subsidies were limited in regard to expenditure and the quantity of product. In general, the Uruguay Round Agreement on Agriculture brought the regulation of agricultural markets more in line with other products, but did not manage to reduce tariff barriers and liberalize markets, since the average height of agricultural tariffs was still at 61 percent and governments had to do little to adjust domestic policies in accordance with the standards of the agreement (Coleman, Grant, and Josling 2004), even if the Uruguay Round is considered as a global negotiation on domestic policies.

The GATT negotiations, which began with the Uruguay Round of multilateral trade negotiations in 1986, progressed toward the Marrakech Agreement (signed April 15, 1994) and the birth of the WTO, which officially entered into force on January 1, 1995, with no expiration date. The

Marrakech Agreement included the Agreement on Agriculture, which was intended to reform the agricultural sector by addressing the subsidies and high trade barriers that were distorting agricultural trade; this was done by increasing market competition and access, true to its founding neoliberal vision.

In the agricultural sector, neoliberalism meant sharp reductions in tariffs and rising imports of cheap staples, cuts in direct and indirect subsidies for producers — except for a few developed countries that were granted exceptional flexibilities, in particular those in the European Union and the United States — and the streamlining of sanitary and phytosanitary regulations that could constitute nontariff barriers to trade (Edelman and Borras 2016: 30). The emerging transnational policy space in agriculture was part of a broader neoliberal moment generated by the change in the mode of capital accumulation, which shifted from materialism to financial expansion.

Farming, which up until that point had been at the core of key policies for state-building, became just one economic activity among many others: national food security and family farming have since then been challenged by the new context based on global trade that defines normative and policy frameworks on agriculture. The neoliberal framework and the internationalization of the discussion on trading rules led to the ministries of trade and finance influencing the definition of agricultural policies according to the logic of the international trading system and the competitive paradigm. The producers are therefore seen from a different perspective, which takes into consideration the interest of the processing and retail industries. As a result, the different sectors of the national government are almost obliged to coordinate in order to internalize at the domestic level the discussions happening at the global level (Coleman, Grant, and Josling 2004).

Previous governance was rooted in the nation-state, with national self-sufficiency in food being the basis of national security, and farmers creating a bulk of conservative landowners who were embedded in the process of building the nation-state (Coleman, Grant, and Josling 2004). The shift of governance from the national level to a global one, where the corporate sector was organized and pushed for a capital- and technology-intensive model of production in agriculture, profoundly affected national and local farmer organizations, which ultimately reacted to the new state of affairs by organizing themselves into TAMs.

The state withdrawal from support for agriculture coincided with increasing pressure on the control of natural resources through privatization, which affected the most vulnerable part of rural communities, especially the ones working with ecological processes rather than capital- and technology-intensive models of production. The institutional shift generated threats and opportunities for rural populations (Bernstein 2006; McMichael 2009) and caused two trends in rural movements: the further localization of advocacy work, so as to occupy the governance space left by state decentralization, and the internationalization of the work of advocacy and lobbying through horizontal networking. With common targets at the international and local levels, rural organizations built alliances internationally and locally.

In this context, different groups of actors emerged: TNCs and other interest groups on the one side, and TAMs and NGOs on the other. Each side has pushed for the establishment of opposing frameworks of agricultural policies, which in turn are defined in the transnational and contested spaces of the United Nations, WTO, IMF, and World Bank, where both TNCs and TAMs are more or less dominant. In these contested spaces, nation-state governments are the central players in rural development (Borras and Franco 2009; Keohane and Nye 2000), even if their role has been transformed by the triple trends of globalization, decentralization, and privatization. National governments are often the means that groups with conflicting interests use to act in the transnational space of governance (Coleman, Grant, and Josling 2004), which is composed of different processes, information flows, and policymakers connected with regional or national political disputes.

This space transformed the way in which civil society and farmer organizations got organized at the transnational level to act as pressure groups and affect the structures and policy agendas at the national level. Indeed, the partnership approach at the global level has redefined the implementation role of CSOs at the national level, given that the way in which normative and policy frameworks generated at the global level are internalized at the national one has changed the way in which public policies are built in the first place. A clear outcome has been the increasing interdependence between different policy areas that were formerly discussed in different spaces: international trade, intellectual property rights, food security, and biodiversity conservation (Coleman, Grant, and Josling 2004). These different emerging spaces have been summarized in Figure 3.1, dating to 2004, which shows the emerging conflict between intellectual property in international trade (known as TRIPS) and the negotiation over biodiversity conservation.

In June 1992, the Earth Summit, held in Rio de Janeiro, adopted the principle of sustainable development, aiming to preserve the environment while meeting the needs of present and future generations. It also approved the so-called Rio Conventions: the Convention on Biological Diversity, the United Nations Convention to Combat Desertification, and the United Nations Framework Convention on Climate Change. The latter addressed

Figure 3.1 Transnational Policy Space in Agriculture

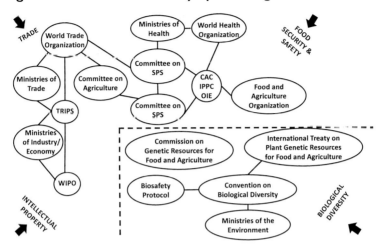

Source: Coleman, Grant, and Josling (2004)

the need for action on climate change by limiting average global temperature increases, and was extended through the 1997 adoption of the Kyoto Protocol, which included legally binding commitments for the developed country parties to reduce emissions. In addition to the Rio Conventions, the summit adopted a global blueprint for sustainable development called *Agenda 21*, which promotes "sustainable agriculture and rural development" with an aim "to increase food production in a sustainable way and enhance food security" (United Nations 1992a).

The Convention on Biological Diversity also hosts an international agreement on biological security. The Cartagena Protocol on Biosafety to the Convention on Biological Diversity, signed in 2000 and ratified by sixty-five states, came into effect in 2003. It is an international agreement that sets out procedures to ensure the safe handling and transboundary transport and use of living modified organisms, which are defined as living organisms that possess a novel combination of genetic material obtained through the use of modern biotechnology, which includes (a) in vitro nucleic acid techniques, including recombinant deoxyribonucleic acid (DNA) and direct injection of nucleic acid into cells or organelles, and (b) the fusion of cells beyond the taxonomic family to overcome natural physiological reproductive or recombination barriers in a technique not used in traditional breeding and selection.

This area of biodiversity and biotech global governance allows broader participation of nonstate actors, and presents a field where opposing interests have been clashing since the signing of the Convention on Biological Diversity in 1992 and the 1994 WTO agreements on agriculture, sanitary and phytosanitary measures, and intellectual property. As a result, two contrasting spheres of authority emerged:

1. The international trade system (including the WTO) and the intellectual property rules known as TRIPS: These are agreements overseen by the World Intellectual Property Organization and the International Union for the Protection of New Varieties of Plants.

2. The Convention on Biological Diversity, its associated biosafety protocol, and the International Treaty on Plant Genetic Resources for Food and Agriculture (ITPGRFA): The latter, which entered into force on June 29, 2004, derives from the voluntary International Undertaking on Plant Genetic Resources, established in 1983 by the Commission on Genetic Resources for Food and Agriculture. The commission hosts the ITPGRFA and is concerned with preserving genetic resources, whether on-site (in situ) or in special collections (ex situ). The ITPGRFA recognizes that the benefits stemming from the use of genetic resources in a place other than the one in which they originated should favour the peasants and Indigenous Peoples who conserve and multiply biodiversity in the fields, by recognizing farmers' rights and increasing their participation in decision-making processes. The benefit-sharing fund coordinated by the ITPGRFA was clearly in conflict with intellectual property as outlined under the TRIPS Agreement.

Figure 3.1 does not fully capture all the existing relationships between the different actors in the transnational policy space in agriculture. Even when considering the institutional level only (and therefore leaving civil society and the private sector out of the analysis), it is crucial to remember that each nation-state participates through different ministries (agriculture, health, economy, trade, environment, and foreign affairs, which is absent from Figure 3.1) and official delegations in various institutional spaces, such as the FAO and the Committee on World Food Security (also not included in Figure 3.1).

From this complex space emerged the institutional guerrilla strategy of TAMs, with various entry points to achieve policy and normative outcomes that could be used in other negotiations. This was made possible by leveraging the lack of coherence and coordination between different delegations of the same government in different spaces of negotiations. A clear example is the utilization of previous negotiations to build the text of the United Nations Declaration on the Rights of Peasants and Other People Working in Rural Areas (United Nations General Assembly 2018), as Article 19 on the right to seeds was based on the ITPGRFA and, in particular, Article 9 on farmers' rights.

The new space of transnational governance of agriculture, shaped by financialization and neoliberal policies, contained an inherent dichotomy between two spheres: one related to intellectual property rights, international trade, and industrial agriculture, and the other related to collective and community rights, public policies, and peasant agriculture. The renewed relevance of the transnational space and this constitutive dichotomy were the conditions for the differentiation of TAMs and the emergence of new formations of them.

In this context, it is important to focus on paragraph 32 of *Agenda 21* (United Nations 1992a), which recognizes farmers as major actors whose activities have strong ties to environmental and developmental issues. It incorporated points made in the secretary-general's report to the 47th General Assembly of the United Nations of May 28, 1992, which emphasized the central role that farmers' organizations, mainly through service provision to their members, should play in the policies of governments and international agencies:

> Organizations of farmers, including agricultural cooperators, are key institutions in the revitalization of agriculture and the development of rural areas, and hence to economic revival particularly in Africa, Asia and Latin America. Their role, in terms both of faithfully representing farmers' views, and of providing practical services to their members, appears often to have been given less attention by Governments and international agencies than they deserve, and consequently their potential has not been fully utilized. Seeking farmers' views through consultations with farmers' representative organizations, and encouraging and supporting the latter in their efforts to provide services to their members are prerequisites for sustainable rural development. The current absence of consultation of farmers, including cooperators, by researchers, is a serious constraint upon accumulation of relevant knowledge and successful diffusion of innovation. (United Nations 1992b: 19)

The discussion of using the full potential of farmers' organizations to develop rural areas can be read in connection with the withdrawal of the nation-state from public policies, and in particular from the agricultural sector, in the neoliberal age. In this case, the squeeze of the nation-state (Edelman and Borras 2016) from above (global governance perspective) and from below (local governance and decentralization perspective) in addition to the budget cuts in agricultural policies further hindered building partnerships with farmers' organizations as an important tool to convey and directly implement new agricultural policies in rural areas.

It is worth noting that TAMs have been in existence since the late nineteenth century (Edelman and Borras 2016), with reference to different political traditions (communist, populist, and feminist) and and the primary aim of building solidarity among farmers' organizations beyond nation-state borders. These movements were mainly linked to national governments, which historically supported agriculture as a core policy of the process of nation-state building. As Tarrow (2005) suggests, from the beginning the emergence of international institutions to serve the "collective interest" of nation-states or to govern the Cold War situation and national independence processes created incentives for transnational activism.

One of the oldest TAMs was the International Federation of Agricultural Producers (IFAP), which was established in 1946 to bring together national farmer organizations to advocate for farmers' interests at the global level, mainly as a private sector counterpart of the FAO. Indeed, IFAP members participated on various occasions in governmental delegations (Edelman and Borras 2016). IFAP considered the potential of the liberalization of agricultural trade and the wide use of agro-biotechnology to ensure food security, and also organized farmer-to-farmer exchanges on the technology of farming, biotechnology, and information technology. In a court judgement dated November 4, 2010, the Tribunal de Grande Instance de Paris dissolved the organization (International Labour Office 2012). In 2011 it was reconstituted as the Rome-based World Farmers' Organisation (WFO), composed of fifty-four organizations claiming to represent 1.5 billion farmers from fifty-four countries all over the world (McKeon 2009).

Another relevant TAM is the International Federation of Organic Agriculture Movements (IFOAM), which was founded in 1972 as an international umbrella organization for the organic world, uniting a diverse range of stakeholders to coordinate the different actions at the national level and to enable the exchange of scientific and experimental knowledge about organic agriculture. In the 1980s the IFOAM structure started to grow with the establishment of a central office, and the federation started to participate in key United Nations fora, such as the FAO, International Fund for Agricultural Development, World Food Programme, United Nations Framework

Convention on Climate Change, United Nations Committee on World Food Security, United Nations Conference on Trade and Development, United Nations Environment Programme, and the United Nations Convention to Combat Desertification. Nowadays, IFOAM has more than 754 affiliates in 116 countries and collects certified organic data from 160 countries with over 80 million hectares of certified land.

At the beginning of the 1990s, the new space of transnational governance of agriculture reshaped the existing TAMs according to the new priorities and processes developing in the international space, which was in turn reshaped by the TAMs: civil society at the international level built new norms and institutional arrangements, contributing to the emergence of a space of global governance as a central actor. Thus, in 1993, in the context of increasing the role of farmers' organizations in transnational spaces, forty-six peasants' organizations met in Mons, Belgium, to "define a progressive alternative to the further liberalization of agriculture and food reflected in the Uruguay Round of the General Agreement on Tariffs and Trade (GATT)" (Vía Campesina 2006).

The result was the creation of Vía Campesina, a transnational peasant space defending a peasant-based agricultural model (relying on family labour and not the capitalization of farming) focused on the principles of social justice, environmental sustainability, and cultural diversity and strengthening local struggles over access and control to natural and productive resources such as land, credit, seeds, and water (Vía Campesina 2006). In doing so, the peasants' organizations distanced themselves from the conservative vision of IFAP, which supports privatization, capitalization, and export-oriented policies in agriculture in consultation and negotiation with the WTO, the OECD, and the World Bank (Karl 1996). Desmarais (2007: 18) notes "the majority of farm and peasant organizations that gathered in Mons in 1993 did not recognize IFAP as the legitimate voice of peasant and small-scale farmers. Many had direct experience with IFAP organizations at the national level."

Vía Campesina positioned itself by asking the WTO to withdraw from agriculture regulation and asking national governments to promote people's food sovereignty, which was defined as "the right to produce food on our own territory" (Desmarais 2002), by implementing agrarian reform, stopping trade liberalization, defending biodiversity and genetic resources, improving gender relations, migrant farmworkers' rights, and human rights in rural areas, and overall promoting policies for sustainable peasant agriculture. During the last stages of the WTO negotiations in 1994 in Geneva, Vía Campesina had more than five thousand farmers marching in the city over the GATT (Desmarais 2002).

The foundation of Vía Campesina and other TAMs supporting food sovereignty was the outcome of a process that was over ten years in the making, in which rural organizations engaged in numerous horizontal organizational exchanges all over the globe, to learn about what was happening in each country as a result of the IMF structural adjustment programs and the incumbent free trade agreements, and at the same time how farming peoples were reacting, their strategies, and which alternatives they were building. These exchanges were at the core of the consolidation of a transnational movement defending peasant livelihoods and modes of existence. Vía Campesina comprises 182 local and national organizations across eighty-one countries, representing about 200 million farmers and their demands for social justice. Along with Vía Campesina, many other TAMs defending a peasant model of production emerged between the mid-1990s and the beginning of the 2000s (see the Appendix for a full listing of TAMs).

The new space of consultation between farmers' organizations and international institutions, which was designed at the forty-seventh session of the United Nations General Assembly and the Earth Summit in Rio, was expected to be occupied by IFAP as the traditional organization representing family farming at the United Nations, the WTO, and World Bank. This was reflected in IFAP's statute, which identified among its objectives that of speaking on behalf of the world farmers — "virtually all the agricultural producers in the industrialised countries and several hundred million farmers in the developing countries" (IFAP 1995: 21) — in meetings with governments. Further, the *Contribution of Co-operative Enterprises and the International Co-operative Movement to Implementation of UN AGENDA 21* (International Co-operative Alliance and the United Nations Department for Policy Coordination and Sustainable Development 1995) reaffirmed the role of IFAP in the global governance space. Most of IFAP's efforts at the United Nations level were directed toward strengthening organizations of small farmers, landless tenants and labourers, other small producers, fisherfolk, and community-based and workers' cooperatives, as reaffirmed by the World Summit for Social Development in Copenhagen in 1995. Indeed, in 1994 IFAP published a statement entitled *Farmers for a Sustainable Future: The Leadership Role of Agriculture,* which identified a policy framework allowing agriculture to contribute to a more sustainable society.

Vía Campesina and other TAMs comprising small-scale food producers and supporting food sovereignty aimed to reclaim this space in the global governance of the United Nations, mainly with regard to the interests of peasants from the Global South. "In all the global debates on agrarian policy, the peasant movement has been absent, we have not had a voice," stated Paul Nicholson, a founding leader of Vía Campesina, at the Second International Conference of Vía Campesina in 1996. "The main reason for the very existence of the Vía Campesina is to be that voice and to speak out for the creation of a more just society.… Vía Campesina must defend the 'peasant way' of rural peoples" (Desmarais 2007: 7).

Peasants and other small-scale food producers recognized the impact that neoliberalism was having on peasant and traditional agriculture and on their livelihoods, and organized themselves at the global level through TAMs, supporting the food sovereignty agenda and opposing the capitalization of agriculture by differentiating themselves from other farmers' organizations oriented toward the production of commodities for export and international markets. The "class struggle" divided TAMs into two opposing groups, in the absence of national state policies that traditionally built the national state security, starting with agriculture:

> The rise of significant peasant and farmer movements in many countries in the late twentieth century is an indication of the incompleteness of the transition to capitalism in agriculture. Concretely, the impetus for organizing movements that eventually formed cross-border ties came from the remaining areas of peasant and small-farm agriculture, which large-scale industrial farming had failed or not tried to subordinate or oblige. (Edelman and Borras 2016: 3)

In this sense, TAMs for food sovereignty were reacting to the attempt by capital to further penetrate into the countryside and the consequent proletarianization process under the financialization phase of the capital accumulation cycle after the end of the Bretton Woods agreements.

During the Rio Earth Summit, IFOAM also started to engage systematically in United Nations processes to promote organic agriculture as a possible solution to tackle hunger and climate change while preserving biodiversity. So the new TAMs that emerged in the 1990s were demanding food sovereignty in the space of global governance institutions, and defending small-scale farming and labour intensive models of production to oppose a further transition of agriculture to capitalism, which would foster the polarization of society and the squeezing of the middle class, which in turn would ignite social conflicts in a context of reduced powers for nation-states.

In order to occupy this global governance space with the voice of small-scale food producers, the different TAMs for food sovereignty convened in

Rome for an NGO Forum held parallel to the FAO World Food Summit in 1996, and publicly demanded food sovereignty inside the FAO space. Vía Campesina (2003) notes, "The concept of food sovereignty was developed by Vía Campesina and brought to the public debate during the World Food Summit in 1996 and represents an alternative to neoliberal policies. Since then, that concept has become a major issue of the international agricultural debate, even within the United Nations bodies." The alternative NGO Forum brought together 1,200 CSOs from eighty countries. They rejected the FAO (1996) "Food for All" documents, which promoted more liberal markets to provide food security for all. However, they saw the FAO as an entry point to voice the concerns of peasants and to present other small-scale food producers' demands for public policies. Unlike other global spaces, the FAO was a United Nations body, based on human rights, that worked directly with peasants' organizations. The IPC (2020: 10) observes:

> At this juncture, global civil society and social movements felt FAO to be a politically interesting intergovernmental forum for advocacy, and an alternative to the WTO and international financial institutions such as the World Bank (WB) and the International Monetary Fund (IMF). There were several reasons for this: as a UN body, FAO stood for more-democratic governance with universal membership and, formally, a one country/one vote decision-making process. FAO maintains a specific focus on food and agriculture and a mission to eliminate hunger, a mandate that includes a strong normative dimension and relative openness to the engagement with civil society and rural people's organizations.

Of the numerous global United Nations summits that took place in the 1990s, the 1996 NGO Forum in Rome is highlighted for having social movements and food producers' organizations constitute the majority of the delegates, leading to the adoption of the statement *Profit for Few or Food for All* — though Vía Campesina did not sign it, seeing it as too influenced by NGOs rather than food producers (Desmarais 2002). The statement rejected the World Food Summit's position: "International law must guarantee the right to food, ensuring food sovereignty takes precedence over macro-economic policies and trade liberalization. Food can not be considered [simply] as a commodity, because of its social and cultural dimension" (NGO Forum 1996). The NGO Forum asserted the principles of autonomy and self-organization of civil society, which were taken as guiding principles for CSOs' participation in FAO processes in the following decades (see *Reform of the Committee on World Food Security* [FAO 2009] and FAO *Strategy for Partnerships with Civil Society Organizations* [FAO 2013]).

The proposal that came from the NGO Forum included the participation of CSOs in United Nations platforms and at the national level, the understanding of CSOs as food producers not working for profit or in a business-oriented way but rather based on a Chayanovian model of agriculture, *with* the autonomy and self-organization of peasant organizations, and extending those principles to participation in the United Nation platforms. In the new TAMs' vision of food sovereignty, national governments would take responsibility for guaranteeing food security, instead of TNCs and the structural adjustment programs of the IMF and the World Bank, where there is no accountability whatsoever. The request for a Right to Food convention ensuring "that the Right to Food will have precedence over any other international agreements such as the World Trade Organization" (NGO Forum 1996) was strong and concrete. Moreover, public policies would be directed toward local and regional food systems, supporting agroecological and sustainable production.

The Uruguay Round and the Agreement on Agriculture consequently underwent a revision, creating a new international space of discussion with TAMs regarding global food policies, and renewing the class dynamics and the political agenda of the TAMs acting at the global level. The new food sovereignty movement composed of TAMs and supportive NGOs claimed a new space in the United Nations system to discuss public policies in support of peasant agriculture and create new legal and policy frameworks to confront the purely neoliberal agenda of the WTO. Apart from the concrete and immediate results, the coordination among CSOs at a global level can be considered the primary outcome of the World Food Summit (Mulvany 1997), as it gave birth to the food sovereignty movement challenging TNCs, global capital, and international crop institutes.

Further, IFOAM scheduled its board meeting to coincide with the FAO World Food Summit in order to raise concerns, and achieved recognition of the role of organic agriculture in the FAO Rome Declaration on World Food Security. In 1997 IFOAM became officially recognized as a partner of the FAO. In 2002 IFOAM managed to include organic agriculture as a "means of implementation" in the United Nations World Summit on Sustainable Development (Rio+10 Conference) outcome document: "Support voluntary WTO-compatible market-based initiatives for the creation and expansion of domestic and international markets for environmentally friendly goods and services, including organic products, which maximize environmental and developmental benefits through, inter alia, capacity-building and technical assistance to developing countries" (United Nations 2002: 48).

Clearly, the IFOAM lobby was positioned toward defending an organic market in the WTO framework. Two years later IFOAM jointly organized the first World Conference on Organic Seed with the FAO and the International Seed Federation at the FAO headquarters in Rome, concluding that there was a "real need for a consultative process between organic farmers, the seed industry, consumers and civil society organizations on co-existence between GM and organic agriculture" (FAO 2004: 6).

During these years, IFOAM negotiated the inclusion of organic agriculture in the agriculture section of the agreement adopted at the seventh session of the Commission on Sustainable Development in New York City. Also in 1996, Singapore hosted the first WTO Ministerial Conference, in which the European Union pushed for the establishment of four permanent working groups on what were referred to as the Singapore issues: (a) transparency in government procurement — rules to allow foreign companies to participate in nondiscriminatory competitions, (b) trade facilitation (customs issues) — rules that require governments to simplify and reduce the cost of transactions, (c) trade and investment — rules for the investors' rights against any interference from the host country, and (d) trade and competition — rules to ensure fair competition, without distinction between foreign and domestic companies, including for government monopolies.

At the following WTO Ministerial Conference, most developing countries opposed the Singapore issues, but the European Union, Japan, and Korea strongly supported them:

> Some cynics suggest that the Singapore issues are just chaff thrown up by the EU and Japan to disguise their own intransigence over agriculture. Ever since the current round of trade talks was launched in 2001, Japan and the EU have been on the defensive. The Doha round's focus on agricultural liberalisation has forced them to defend some of the most illiberal but well-entrenched systems of agricultural protection in the world. Japan's import tariffs on rice go up to 1,000%, for instance. The EU spends more on annual subsidies for each of its cows than most sub-Saharan Africans earn in a year. Both insist on progress on the Singapore issues as a quid pro quo for long-overdue agricultural reforms that still seem politically beyond them. If poor countries refuse to yield ground, the EU and Japan can blame them for their inflexibility over the Singapore issues, rather than taking the blame for their own inflexibility over agriculture. (*The Economist* 2003)

The 1999 WTO Ministerial Conference in Seattle was suspended due to a march of different social movements, including the TAMs, which blocked the city to protest neoliberal policies, in what is remembered as the Battle of Seattle. Vía Campesina protested in the streets of Geneva and Seattle, reclaiming agriculture from the WTO, as was clearly stated in the statement delivered at events surrounding the WTO ministerial meeting in Seattle in November 1999 (Vía Campesina 1999). In asking to get the WTO out of agriculture, Vía Campesina recognized that food had become a central issue for neoliberal policies and global institutions such as the WTO, IMF, and World Bank, which were destroying family farm economies. Thus, Vía Campesina emphasized the strategy initiated at the World Food Summit in 1996, which included strengthening the new instruments developed within the United Nations system to increase transparency and democratic control and ensure food security and fair trade.

The WTO discussion was supposed to tackle the issue of intellectual property rights and biotechnologies, given the European Commission had refused to consider applications for approval of agricultural biotechnology since 1998. It was decided to reattempt the negotiations at the following Ministerial Conference in November 2001 in Doha, Qatar. These negotiations centred on the Singapore issues and would continue until 2005 to make trade rules more just for developing countries, mainly in regard to opening up agricultural and manufacturing markets, as well as trade in services (General Agreement on Trade in Services) and intellectual property (TRIPS Agreement) regulation. During this period the private sector and the different biotech companies started to reorganize themselves in order to influence the discussions and negotiations: after witnessing the failure of the WTO at the Seattle ministerial meeting, BASF Bayer, Dow, DuPont, FMC, Syngenta, Monsanto, and Sumitomo gave birth in 2001 to CropLife International, an international trade association composed of national and regional agricultural chemical associations.

In the following year, the FAO organized a World Food Summit called Five Years Later, following up on pledges made at the 1996 World Food Summit. Civil society organized a concurrent event, the Forum for Food Sovereignty in Rome, hosting more than seven hundred NGOs and CSOs, as the result of an international consultation and interaction process spanning two years. During the conclusive day of the Five Years Later summit, the IPC delivered a final statement on behalf of the Forum for Food Sovereignty in the presence of the heads of state and governmental delegations. The 2002 declaration, *Food Sovereignty: A Right for All* (NGO/CSO Forum for Food Sovereignty 2002), finally affirmed the leadership of TAMs in the rising food sovereignty movement. In the declaration, TAMs criticized governments' lack of political will to implement the 1996 World Food Summit plan of action. Food sovereignty was presented as the fundamental approach to guaranteeing access to productive resources and ending the neoliberal policies of the World Bank, WTO, and IMF. The aim was to overrule the WTO at Cancun in September 2003.

The CSOs' declaration contested the official statement of the Five Years Later summit, indicating that the neoliberal policies regarding the privatization of natural resources in favour of a few TNCs were the main reason for the failure in implementing the 1996 World Food Summit plan of action. The declaration reaffirmed that food sovereignty was the right of peoples, who should produce food for themselves, and for domestic and local markets, not for export. For this reason, access to land, water, seeds, and other productive resources is essential. This was a clear position against the World Bank, WTO, and IMF. In this context, the IPC was institutionalized and recognized as the space articulating food sovereignty and giving priority to social movements and not NGOs. The FAO recognized the importance of becoming an ally of social movements to change the political attitude of governments in the fight against hunger.

After the Five Years Later summit, the IPC signed a formal agreement with the FAO recognizing the principles of bottom-up participation of CSOs:

> FAO accepts the principles of civil society autonomy and self-organization on which the IPC bases its work and will apply them in all of its relations with NGOs/CSOs.... FAO recognizes the IPC as its principal global civil society interlocutor on the initiatives and themes emerging from WFS:fyl [World Food Summit: Five Years Later] and the NGOs/CSOs Forum of June 2002.... Both parties concur with the need to distinguish between the interests of social movements/non-profit NGOs and those of private sector associations, and to make separate interface arrangements for these two categories of organizations. (Internal document 2003).

Through this agreement, the IPC started to participate in FAO processes as the main interlocutor for CSOs.

As a first act, the IPC participated in the negotiations to draft guidelines for the implementation of the 1996 World Food Summit plan of action. The final recommendations of the Five Years Later summit invited the FAO Council to establish an intergovernmental working group to develop voluntary guidelines to support member states' efforts to realize the right to adequate food. This intergovernmental working group was set up in November 2002, and after two years of negotiation the *Voluntary Guidelines to Support the Progressive Realization of the Right to Adequate Food in the Context of National Food Security* (or *Right to Food Guidelines*) were adopted by the FAO Council in November 2004.

The voluntary guidelines were a soft law approach to having an international nonbinding instrument — that is to say, an international reference for policies on the subject discussed. Ideally, all national governments that want to revise their policies and legislation should make some reference to the voluntary guidelines. The strategy of the food sovereignty movement was to negotiate the guidelines with governments in order to open spaces at a national level and create an international framework to provide access to productive resources such as land, water, seeds, and so forth. This international framework to access natural resources would establish the basis for discussing agroecology beyond a simple model of production, in order to achieve food sovereignty.

In 2003 at the WTO Ministerial Conference in Cancun, which was mainly focused on the Singapore issues, Brazil, China, India, and South Africa formed part of a bloc of over twenty countries (G22) that negotiated jointly on agriculture and did not support any negotiation on the Singapore issues. This illustrated the wide gap between developing and developed countries, particularly the North versus South divide, which was more prominent in agriculture in reference to the European Union's Common Agricultural Policy and the United States' agricultural subsidies (Coleman, Grant, and Josling 2004). Vía Campesina and the World Forum of Fish Harvesters and Fishworkers, which were both part of the IPC process in Rome, delivered a statement (Vía Campesina 2003) underlining the failure of the negotiation in Cancun, requesting national governments to protect domestic food production and distribution following a human rights–based approach, and calling upon the FAO, United Nations Conference on Trade and Development, and the International Labour Organization to develop an alternative international framework for food and agriculture.

While the TAMs and some governments who had close ties to their agenda (such as Brazil under President Lula, and in some ways China and India) were blocking the WTO negotiations on agriculture, after the approval of the *Right to Food Guidelines* the IPC contributed to the preparation and organization of the 2006 International Conference on Agrarian Reform and Rural Development, which promoted agrarian reform as a crucial element to fight hunger and poverty and opened up the way to the negotiation of the *Voluntary Guidelines on the Responsible Governance of Tenure of Land,*

Fisheries and Forests in the Context of National Food Security (also called the *Voluntary Guidelines on Tenure*), which were adopted by the Committee on World Food Security in May 2012 (Gaarde 2017; Margulis and Duncan 2016). During the International Conference on Agrarian Reform and Rural Development, the IPC facilitated and organized a parallel NGO forum, which was attended by an estimated five hundred civil society leaders representing different groups comprised of peasants, pastoralists, nomads, Indigenous Peoples, and subsistence fisherfolk, among others (Gaarde 2017). At the same time, the TNCs began to lobby the FAO with the support of governments from the Global North, and CSOs' participation in these spaces was difficult at the regional and national levels.

Vía Campesina launched the idea of organizing a World Forum for Food Sovereignty. At the IPC general meeting in November 2005, it was decided to allocate more than six hundred seats to different food producer constituencies (farmers, fisherfolk, Indigenous Peoples, pastoralists, women's groups, workers, environmentalists, consumers, NGOs, and youth) from around the world in order to establish a common definition of food sovereignty and collectively build strategies based on the concrete practices of delegates. The Forum for Food Sovereignty, also called Nyéléni, was held in Mali in February 2007, with discussion focused on the recognition of food sovereignty. Eleven years after unveiling the concept of food sovereignty, it was time to better define and clarify the implications that food and agricultural policies had at the regional and national levels. Going beyond previous declarations, the forum produced the six principles of food sovereignty, giving concrete indications for their implementation (see Table 3.1).

In that same year, the food price crisis put food policies at the top of the global governance agenda. Relaunching a proposal from the 1996 World Food Summit to have a global convention on food security, the IPC, alongside the FAO and a regional group of Latin American governments, proposed a reform of the Committee on World Food Security such that it would become an inclusive forum for policy dialogue and coherence on food security and nutrition. This proposal defeated one to have the New York–based United Nations and G8 at the head of world food governance. The reform was adopted in 2009, and in the following years the IPC helped create the Committee on World Food Security's Civil Society Mechanism, based on the principles of autonomy and self-organization for social movements. The first negotiation to involve the Civil Society Mechanism was about the drafting of the *Voluntary Guidelines on Tenure*. After the approval of the guidelines, following the momentum of the Committee on World

Food Security reform, the FAO also entered into a new phase of including civil society in its processes (Gaarde 2017; McKeon 2016).

Once the *Right to Food Guidelines* had been established, the TAMs aimed to discuss access to different natural and productive resources to transition toward agroecology; a food system built on access to productive resources was a tool to reach food sovereignty. The reform of the Committee on World Food Security provided an opportunity to advance this agenda, but after the election of Gerda Verburg of the Netherlands as the Committee on World Food Security chair in 2013, the committee went through a bureaucratization process affecting its agenda and emerging priorities, which no longer reflected the priorities of the TAMs for food sovereignty. The blocking of the TAMs' agenda for the following year corresponded to a veto on any discussion on genetic resources or agroecology in the Multi-Year Programme of Work Open-Ended Working Group. The same slow demolition of the reform impacted the WFO (formerly IFAP), which wound up participating in the Committee on World Food Security without going through its official mechanisms (Private Sector and Civil Society Mechanisms) (Duncan and Zanella 2016; McKeon 2015, 2017)

In 2012–13, the IPC worked toward the approval of the FAO *Strategy for Partnership with CSOs* (FAO 2013), which would institutionalize the CSOs' participation in the FAO normative bodies and in the regular program. The IPC went on to achieve the approval of the *Voluntary Guidelines for Securing Sustainable Small-Scale Fisheries in the Context of Food Security and Poverty Eradication*; the global and regional symposia on agroecology, which resulted in the FAO Scaling Up Agroecology Initiative; the implementation process for Article 9 of the ITPGRFA, addressing farmers' collective rights to seeds; and active participation in the FAO regional offices and processes.

Table 3.1 Six Principles of Food Sovereignty

NYÉLÉNI 2007: FORUM FOR FOOD SOVEREIGNTY DEFINITION OF FOOD SOVEREIGNTY (FROM THE DECLARATION OF NYÉLÉNI)
Food sovereignty is the right of peoples to healthy and culturally appropriate food produced through ecologically sound and sustainable methods, and their right to define their own food and agricultural systems. It puts the aspirations and needs of those who produce, distribute and consume food at the heart of food systems and policies rather than the demands of markets and corporations. It defends the interests and inclusion of the next generation. It offers a strategy to resists and dismantle the current corporate trade and food regime, and directions for food, farming, pastoral and fisheries systems determined to local producers and users. Food sovereignty prioritises local and national economies and markets and empowers peasant and family farmer-driven agriculture, artisanal-fishing, pastoralist-led grazing, and food production, distribution and consumption based on environmental, social and economic stainability. Food sovereignty promotes transparent trade that guarantees just incomes to all people as well as the rights of consumers to control their food and nutrition. It ensures that the rights to use and manage lands, territories, waters, seeds, livestock and biodiversity are in the hands of those of us who produce food. Food sovereignty implies new social relations free of oppression and inequality between men and women, peoples, racial groups, social and economic classes and generations.

SIX PRINCIPLES OF FOOD SOVEREIGNTY (FROM SYNTHESIS REPORT)

	Food Sovereignty:	is FOR	is AGAINST
1.	Focuses on Food for People:	Food sovereignty puts the right to sufficient, healthy and culturally appropriate food for all individuals, peoples and communities, including those who are hungry, under occupation, in conflict zones and marginalised, at the centre of food, agriculture, livestock and fisheries policies;	and *rejects* the proposition that food is just another commodity or component for international agri-business.
2.	Values Food Providers:	Food sovereignty values and supports the contributions, and respects the rights, of women and men, peasants and small scale family farmers, pastoralists, artisanal fisherfolk, forest dwellers, indigenous peoples and agricultural and fisheries workers, including migrants, who cultivate, grow, harvest and process food;	and *rejects* those policies, actions and programmes that undervalue them, threaten their livelihoods and eliminate them.

3.	Localises Food Systems:	Food sovereignty brings food providers and consumers closer together; puts providers and consumers at the centre of decision-making on food issues; protects food providers from the dumping of food and food aid in local markets; protects consumers from poor quality and unhealthy food, inappropriate food aid and food tainted with genetically modified organisms;	and *rejects* government structures, agreements and practices that depend on and promote unsustainable and inequitable international trade and give power to remote and unaccountable corporations.
4.	Puts Control Locally:	Food sovereignty places control over territory, land, grazing, water, seeds, livestock and fish populations on local food providers and respects their rights. They can use and share them in socially and environmentally sustainable ways which conserve diversity; it recognizes that local territories often cross geopolitical borders and ensures the right of local communities to inhabit and use their territories; it promotes positive interaction between food providers in different regions and territories and from different sectors that helps resolve internal conflicts or conflicts with local and national authorities;	and *rejects* the privitisation through laws, commercial contracts and intellectual property rights regimes.
5.	Builds Knowledge and Skills:	Food sovereignty builds on the skills and local knowledge of food providers and their local organisations that conserve, develop and manage localised food production and harvesting systems, developing appropriate research systems to support this and passing on this wisdom to future generations;	and *rejects* technologies that undermine, threaten or contaminate these, e.g. genetic engineering.
6.	Works with Nature:	Food sovereignty uses the contributions of nature in diverse, low external input agroecological production and harvesting methods that maximise the contribution of ecosystems and improve resilience and adaptation, especially in the face of climate change; it seeks to *"heal the planet so that the planet may heal us."*	and *rejects* methods that harm beneficial ecosystem functions, that depend on energy intensive monocultures and livestock factories, destructive fishing practices and other industrialised production methods, which damage the environment and contribute to global warming.

Source: Nyéléni Declaration (2007)

Climate Change and Family Farming

A Confrontation at the Agroecological Frontier

As seen in the previous chapter, the Rio Conventions are at the core of the policy frameworks supporting sustainable agriculture and collective rights in accessing natural resources. To understand recent FAO processes, it is worth considering the impact of the climate change policy framework on them. COP21 and COP22 exposed the Green Revolution and industrial agriculture models of production as climate-inefficient (Altieri and Nicholls 2020). This narrative on climate change is important to understand the policy processes that involved radical TAMs in the FAO under José Graziano da Silva's two terms as director-general (2012–19), before which he had served as minister for food security in the Brazilian government of Lula.

In this period, the FAO gained an even more prominent role in the complex and multilevel discussion of the transnational space of governance of agriculture. The most relevant FAO policy dialogue processes for this research are the International Year of Family Farming (2014), the agroecology symposia (2014–18), and the symposia on biotechnologies, innovation, and digitalization (2016–19). These FAO policy frameworks were subject to intense negotiation by the TAMs, organized through the IPC, which defended agroecology as a pathway toward the realization of food sovereignty and the transformation of the food system (IPC 2015). At the same time, the corporate sector tried to use the paradigm shift in favour of family farming and agroecology to capture peasant agriculture through NBTs and the regulation of DSI in order to appropriate world biodiversity.

Indeed, the 2014 celebration of the International Year of Family Farming and the first discussion regarding the recognition of agroecology as a normative framework, in the broader context of climate change negotiations, indirectly opened up a new conflict over the possible appropriation of the world's biodiversity — the founding pillar of not only peasant family farming but also the agroecological model of production — by dispossession through patenting. This appropriation would allow further capitalist penetration in the agroecological frontier and the inclusion of external frontiers in capitalist agriculture.

To understand this situation, we should start with the Paris Agreement, which was adopted on December 12, 2015. Building on the work initiated under the Convention on Biological Diversity, it seeks to accelerate and intensify the actions and investment needed for a sustainable low-carbon future. Its central aim is to strengthen the global response to the threat of climate change by keeping the global temperature rise this century well under 2 degrees Celsius above preindustrial levels and to pursue efforts to limit the temperature increase even further to 1.5 degrees Celsius. An OECD background document for COP21 recognizes that agriculture is accountable for a significant share of greenhouse gas emissions: 17 percent produced through agricultural activities and an additional 7 to 14 percent produced through land-use changes (European Environment Agency 2015). Furthermore, according to the European Environment Agency (2015):

> Agriculture both contributes to climate change and is affected by climate change. The EU needs to reduce its greenhouse-gas emissions from agriculture and adapt its food-production system to cope with climate change. But climate change is only one of many pressures on agriculture. Faced with growing global demand and competition for resources, the EU's food production and consumption need to be seen in a broader context, linking agriculture, energy, and food security.

The weight of agriculture in the Paris Agreement is felt in the preamble, which acknowledges "the fundamental priority of safeguarding food security and ending hunger, and the particular vulnerabilities of food production systems to the adverse impacts of climate change" (United Nations Framework Convention on Climate Change 2016: 2). In addition, the preamble includes references to human rights, development, gender, ecosystems, and biodiversity, all of which are of key importance to agriculture. The role of farmers and smallholders in tackling climate change was also reiterated in 2016 during COP22 in Marrakech, which "highlighted the active engagement of local communities as a key factor for the successful implementation of adaptation measures in agriculture. Some Parties expressed a preference for bottom-up projects that are designed by farmers groups or other local initiatives and employ the traditional know-how and practical wisdom of those stakeholder groups" (Subsidiary Body for Scientific and Technological Advice 2016: 8).

Thus, the climate change policy framework discredits the Green Revolution and the industrial agriculture models of production as climate-inefficient, even if there is no change to the narrative on the necessity of boosting food production for the estimated global population of up to nine billion inhabitants in 2050:

> The UN Environmental Program's [sic] recent report on the "environmental food crisis" (Nellemann et al. 2009) predicts, inter alia, climate change–driven reduction in cropland by 8–20 per cent by mid-century; mounting pressures on aquifers and above all glaciers, signalling looming water scarcity; the proliferation of invasive species, and rising biological resistance to pesticides and herbicides; rising fertilizer prices, and their declining effect on yields; escalating competition for arable land from agrofuels (already one-third of the US maize crop in 2008); and, perhaps most ominously, "an absolute decline in the productive land area (Net Primary Productivity) across 12 percent" of the planet, with the areas most affected home to nearly one-fifth of world population — all of which will be amplified still further by climate change and the mounting "risk of abrupt and major irreversible changes" (ibid., 40, 43). The progress of global warming is, moreover, already implicated in the yield suppression of major cereal crops (Cline 2007). (Moore 2010c: 400)

This narrative on climate change is important for understanding the attempt to use the NBTs and the regulation of DSI to appropriate the world's biodiversity. The debate about regulating NBTs has been quite strong. NBT promoters claim the technology is exempt from GMO regulations since no alien DNA is inserted into the plant. Instead, the plant's genome is rearranged, as could occur naturally. Paolo De Castro, vice-chairman of the Agriculture Committee in the European Parliament, stated in 2017 that "breeding techniques which do not involve genomic modification from one species to another, and simply accelerate modifications that could happen in nature, should not be considered as the old-fashioned genetic modifications" (White 2017). So NBTs were presented as an opportunity to protect biodiversity and intensify food production while also reducing the input of pesticides and the effects of climate change.

The International Year of Family Farming in 2014 shifted understandings of family farming. The legacy document recognizes family farming as "the most prevalent form of agriculture in the world," the one feeding the world: "There are more than 570 million farms in the world out of which more than 500 million are family farms. Statistics show that they produce more than 80 percent of the world's food in value terms" (FAO 2014a: 1). Further, "while there is diversity, the vast majority of world's family farms are small or very small. Family farms are collectively the largest source of employment worldwide. Family Farming is much more than a mode of food production, it is also a way of life" (FAO 2014a: 1). (It is worth noting this concept of family farming does not derive from the work of Alexander V. Chayanov [1966, 1989], a Russian agrarian economist who originated the concept and theory of family farming, where a farm household entirely reliant on family labour works for a living, not a profit.)

The FAO key fact infographics for the International Year of Family Farming break these numbers down further: (a) Family and individual farms make up more than 90 percent of total farms and occupy only 70–80 percent of farmland, yet they produce 80 percent of the world's food and (b) 72 percent of family farms take up less than 1 hectare, and only 6 percent have more than 5 hectares of farmland (FAO n.d.a). The International Year of Family Farming illustrated the centrality of family farming for food security and recognized its efficiency as a model of production, contesting the mainstream narrative about family farming (FAO 2016b; World Bank 2008). While smallholders were feeding the world in a sustainable way, the mainstream vision saw them as inefficient and their model of production as needing improvement to reduce their vulnerability to climate change.

The International Year of Family Farming was therefore a crucial process for shifting the narrative on family farming to one closer to the Chayanovian approach of van der Ploeg (2010: 14):

> In peasant agriculture the longing for better incomes translates, both at the level of the single households and at the level of the sector as a whole, into increased production. When all the relevant conditions are the same, peasant farming produces more food in a given area than entrepreneurial farming.... The well-known inverse relationship (under which small peasant units produce more per unit of land than far larger entrepreneurial or capitalist units) and the law of diminishing returns (implying that intensification meets clear limits beyond which agrarian involution will emerge) are clear examples of this.

According to this new approach, peasant production was considered the most efficient way to feed the world and was no longer perceived as an inefficient and suboptimal part of agriculture. This vision of peasant farming was closely linked to the closure of the great frontier, implying a better allocation of resources (internal frontier) and the inclusion of new areas (external frontiers):

> Entrepreneurial and capitalist farming tend to limit themselves to fertile deltas, where the ecological, infrastructural, and social conditions meet the assumptions and requirements of modernized farming. This marginalizes other areas, which come to lay barren. Peasant agriculture can revitalize these uncompetitive areas and make them productive once again....
>
> Ecological capital supplies the main natural resources, co-production allows for steady but ongoing improvements in technical efficiency (the ratio between total production and the resources used), and self-provisioning implies that all the technical and social means required to convert natural resources into production are available. Through such mechanisms, food production can be sustained over long periods and steadily enlarged. Following this pattern, the capacity to respond to increased demand for food is an endogenous quality: growth is not necessarily triggered by external interventions. (van der Ploeg 2010: 16, 23–24)

This new narrative could help restructure current food production on a smaller scale, with more integration in global value chains (internal frontier) — but mainly it offers the opportunity to expand the external frontier of capitalism based on the core of peasant farming: unpatented (for now) world biodiversity. This possibility emerged from coupling the outcomes of the International Year of Family Farming and the discussion on agroecology, in the framework of climate change discussions, and including the NBTS as a Trojan horse to allow the appropriation of world biodiversity through patenting.

In fact, in 2014, the FAO also organized an International Symposium on Agroecology for Food Security and Nutrition as a technical dialogue. The symposium allowed participants "to share experiences and build the evidence base on agroecology," "[reach] consensus on the priorities for achieving more sustainable food systems through agroecology," and "[endorse the] FAO's role in supporting further implementation and promotion of agroecological approaches" (FAO, n.d.b). During the final plenary session, the governments of Brazil and Senegal offered to host a symposium on agroecology in their region to better understand agroecological practices and experiences there. As a result, immediately after the end of the international symposium, Brazil and France, in close contact with CSOs, supported the FAO mainstreaming of agroecology in its regular program as a tool to be offered as technical assistance to the member states. The FAO symposia and dialogues on agroecology were framed as a technical rather than political discussion in order to avoid any conflict in the follow-up process.

The IPC strategy was to discuss access to different natural and productive resources (e.g., land, seeds, water, markets) in the Committee on World Food Security and in the FAO committees and from these outcomes try to contribute to the agroecology discussion. However, after the approval of the *Voluntary Guidelines on Tenure* in the extra session of the Committee on World Food Security in May 2012, any attempt to discuss genetic resources or agroecology was rejected by the North American and Pacific regions, despite the support of the African and Latin American Regions. Consequently, after a series of informal talks, the governments of France and Brazil, with the support of the IPC and its allies, decided to strongly support an FAO technical discussion on agroecology with a dedicated process (two international symposia and at least one for each region) in order to have enough case studies and inputs to then mainstream it in the FAO regular program. (Indeed, the outcomes of the Second International Symposium on Agroecology were presented to the FAO Committee on Agriculture in October 2018 [FAO 2019a] and then sent to the FAO Council in order to include agroecology in the FAO's strategic plan for the years to come.)

The First International Symposium on Agroecology in 2014 saw strong engagement on behalf of social movements under the leadership of the IPC in the steering committee, and many panellists attended each session of the discussion. During the closing of the symposium, the governments of Brazil and Senegal committed to organizing regional dialogues on agroecology in Latin America and Africa. Following these statements, the IPC announced that it was going to organize a global meeting of CSOs in Nyéléni, Mali, in order to find a common understanding of agroecology and establish some coordination between the different regional discussions in Asia, Latin America, Africa, and Europe. After the end of the First International Symposium, Vía Campesina had denounced the attempt to reduce agroecology to just "a few new tools for the toolbox of industrial agriculture" (Vía Campesina 2014). The main purpose of the Nyéléni International Forum for Agroecology in 2015 was to define agroecology as a complete alternative to industrial agriculture.

The final declaration of the International Forum for Agroecology, dated February 27, 2015, defines agroecology as "a way of life and the language of Nature" and "not a mere set of technologies or production practices. It cannot be implemented the same way in all territories" (IPC 2015: 2). Evidently, the social dimension of different territories and communities and their customary rights (translated into collective rights in modern law) is at the core of agroecology, which cannot be reduced to an agronomic technique. The rejection of the commodification of life and of global markets *challenged and transformed structures of power in society* by demonstrating that the ethical and solidarity basis of agroecology was incompatible with capitalist agriculture, which had caused the climate crisis and inability to feed the world due to its internal contradictions, and the depletion of the natural resources needed for food production.

This declaration was catalyzed by some governments' attempts to narrow down agroecology to a simple technique and by FAO Director-General Graziano da Silva's closing remarks at the First International Symposium on Agroecology that "today a window was opened in what for 50 years has been the Cathedral of the Green Revolution" (Vía Campesina 2014) and that the FAO should be an open and neutral space to ensure a policy dialogue on agricultural policies and tools, including GMOs. The informal talks made it clear that this opening to discuss GMOs was the result of strong pressure from governments of the Global North (mainly the United States, the Netherlands, and Australia) and CropLife International to counterbalance the process of agroecology with a similar one of biotechnology.

So in 2015, after the Nyéléni International Forum for Agroecology, each FAO region organized a regional symposium on agroecology (with the exception of Europe, which focused on COP21), shedding light on most of the outcomes from the regional processes of agroecology. In contrast, in 2016 the FAO held the International Symposium on the Role of Agricultural Biotechnologies in Sustainable Food Systems and Nutrition with the financial support of USAID, the Netherlands, and Australia. The biotech symposium was quite problematic since the FAO did not confirm the availability of interpretation services in three languages and support for CSO participation until a few days before the meeting. So the IPC had only one panellist, with a small delegation participating from the floor. For these reasons Vía Campesina (2015) published a critical statement the day before the symposium, which created some tensions. The main outcome of the symposium was the promotion of biotechnologies that were compatible with agroecology, in order to avoid the mutual exclusion of the two approaches and to integrate family farming, agroecology, and its work with biodiversity and nature within capitalist agriculture.

As was expected by the IPC and in particular by Vía Campesina, the governments of the United States, Canada, and Australia and the private sector reacted to the FAO processes that were mainstreaming family farming and agroecology, by boiling down the social and economic dimensions (incompatible with capitalist accumulation) into a technique that could be integrated within a capitalist model of production. Louise Fresco, a professor from Wageningen University and Research in the Netherlands and a member of the symposium's steering committee, said during the closing plenary session:

> As stated very clearly in this symposium, the biotechnology toolbox needs to be linked to the agroecology toolbox and coordinated in a comprehensive and inclusive fashion. This new linkage will be a real challenge technically as it requires an interdisciplinary approach and it will be necessary for governments to engage many different sectors and not just the ministry of agriculture....
>
> What is important here is that we move the discussion past the black and white view of patenting versus open access and make sure that small farmers, poor countries and poor consumers do not become the victims of this debate....
>
> One issue that was only briefly mentioned during this symposium is that of open data or big data. As genetic data becomes available online we can combine it with climate data and soil data to form an enormously powerful tool to fine-tune research efforts as well as farmers' activities to get the best out of the environments in which they work. However, that data is valuable and so it must be considered in terms of intellectual property rights. How should we deal with this massive data? This an issue that we have barely begun to address.
>
> What does all this mean for FAO? By hosting this symposium, FAO has positioned itself right in the heart of a new debate on biotechnology. This is very different from the old black versus white, pro versus contra GMO debate. It is a debate which goes beyond just talking about small farmers but instead addresses the entire food chain. It also goes beyond science and involves governments, civil society and the private sector. (FAO 2016a: 257–58)

Fresco presented a manifesto for the inclusion of NBTS and DSI in FAO policies: there was a clear will to overrule the definition of living modified organisms in the Cartagena Protocol, consider NBTS as non-GMOs, and use the DSI of genetic resources (not covered in this book but extensively discussed in the ITPGRFA and the Convention on Biological Diversity) with an open-source approach to generate a new policy framework and move beyond all of the conflicts that had blocked the old GMOs.

FAO Director-General Graziano da Silva's closing statement recaptured the suggestion to integrate biotechnologies in agroecology:

> No one single tool, technology or approach will provide a complete solution for all the problems we have. Responding to the urgent and diverse challenges of the twenty-first century will require a combination of responses. And our responses will also evolve as our knowledge advances. Ladies and gentlemen, we have unlocked the door to discuss and analyse how agroecology and biotechnology can live together, and, perhaps, be used as complementary options. This is an outstanding achievement of this symposium. It opens a window of opportunity for the development of new technologies that could make agricultural sectors more sustainable in the years to come. We have also agreed that tools and approaches must be useful and accessible for farmers, in particular family farmers....
>
> Some presentations made in this symposium highlighted the possible contributions of new biotechnologies, both low-tech and high-tech, that could best serve the interests of farmers, in particular family farmers. Several presentations also reiterated that agricultural biotechnologies are much broader than genetically modified organisms. (FAO 2016a: 261)

An underlying complementarity between agricultural biotechnologies and agroecology was emphasized in a symposium side event called New Breeding Technologies for Smallholders' Challenges, organized by the Dutch Ministry of Economic Affairs, where speakers recommended not regulating NBTS. No evidence of a risk to the environment and health exists, said Niels Louwaars, director of Plantum, the Dutch association for the plant reproduction material sector. And in the absence of an alien genome, there is no basis for a safety risk analysis, stated Rene Smulders, business unit manager of plant breeding at Wageningen University and Research. Implicitly, this open-source approach is directed toward the genetic resources that are not protected by intellectual property rights, which are precisely those that farmers and peasants are using for their agroecological production. The thrust of the discussion toward smallholders was clearly captured on Capacity4dev, the European Commission's online knowledge-sharing platform that connects development professionals, where a user observed "an emerging awareness that biotechnologies are broader than GMOs and that biotechnologies and agroecology have to live together and be more integrated if agriculture is to be more sustainable particularly for smallholder farmers. FAO is ready to play a role as a platform for further developing this integration" (Former Capacity4dev Member 2022).

As the only IPC panellist in the biotech symposium, Guy Kastler (2016: 201) from Vía Campesina addressed the failure of GMOs to preserve the yields of the Green Revolution, and condemned the attempt to rewrite the definition of GMOs in the Cartagena Protocol as any in vitro nucleic acid techniques:

> Facing consumers' rejection of GMOs, the industry has come up with new techniques of genetic modification and is now willing to have them escape GMO regulations. Those genetic engineering techniques aim at modifying *in vitro* the genes of cropped plants' cells. They undoubtedly produce living modified organisms as defined by the Cartagena Protocol on Biosafety. Under the pretext that some of those techniques leave no trace of the genetic material introduced in the cells to modify their genome, the industry is willing to have those plants not qualified as GMOs in order to escape the international rules of the Cartagena Protocol and the mandatory labelling, risk assessment and follow-up as imposed by many national regulations. It therefore tries to modify the GMO definition in order to reduce it to the insertion of recombinant DNA found in the final product. It is totally unacceptable that FAO endorses in its own publications this obvious violation of the only accepted international definition of GMOs given by the Cartagena Protocol.
>
> This new move from industry is all the more perverse by allowing it to patent genes without distinguishing them from naturally occurring genes in peasants' seeds and in seeds stored in gene banks. The entire cropped biodiversity available is this way being brought under the control of a few multinationals owning the biggest patent portfolios.

This statement refers to the fact that NBTs have the potential to appropriate crop diversity in its entirety. In order to be effective, this appropriation of biodiversity should work in peasant agriculture, which constitutes most family farming (80 percent of the food consumed) and is mostly based on agroecology, working with nature according to ecological principles. This was clarified even further in the side talks with the governments of the Global South, which could not participate in large numbers during the technical discussions as they usually did during official FAO meetings. Contrarily, other TAMs such as the WFO supported the inclusion of NBTs in family farming. "Farmers and plant breeders need to be increasingly innovative to deal with the challenge of feeding a growing world population with limited resources and increasingly variable weather events, ranging from floods to droughts," stated Thor Kofoed of Copa-Cogeca, which unites the Committee of Professional Agricultural Organisations (Copa) with the General Confederation of Agricultural Cooperatives (Cogeca) and is essentially the European component of the WFO (Hortidaily 2017).

The peasant component of family farming constitutes a reserve of natural resources and production models that are not yet fully captured inside the internal frontier of capital accumulation; therefore, they represent a great opportunity for capital penetration in agriculture to expand the agroecological frontiers and to lower the cost of food production through an innovative technique, which, more than the promise to increase yields, will allow the appropriation of biodiversity and all farming systems. This corresponds to what Moore defines as an organizational revolution in agriculture. This new narrative built upon climate change, family farming, and agroecology assumes that the best way to intervene in this agroecological model of production — where family farmers are feeding the world and are (subtly) the most sustainable and efficient food producers — is to stress why family farmers need the support of biotechnologies such as NBTs.

In order to understand the inclusion of biotech in family farming, the FAO's 2014 and 2016 *State of Food and Agriculture* reports are helpful. The 2014 report, *The State of Food and Agriculture: Innovation in Family Farming* (FAO 2014b), recognizes that farmers have often been seen as an obstacle to the development of a country and have been denied government support, even though they are central to solving the hunger crisis. They need support to access technologies that bolster sustainable increases in productivity without unduly raising risks and improved participation in value chains, since they are more vulnerable to the effects of climate change.

The 2016 report, *The State of Food and Agriculture: Climate Change, Agriculture and Food Security* (FAO 2016b), focuses more on the effects of climate change for smallholders and the support they need to adapt. It acknowledges agroecology and sustainable intensification as integrated approaches for yield improvement and resilience-building, suggesting the depletion of natural resources caused by conventional agriculture can be tackled through diversified food productions systems that are harmonized with ecological processes. Small farmers are considered most vulnerable to climate change and the most malnourished, and thus should be supported to adapt to climate change by innovating to be resilient and increasing production to meet projected food needs by 2050:

> A major finding is that there is an urgent need to support small-holders in adapting to climate change. Farmers, pastoralists, fisherfolk and community foresters depend on activities that are intimately and inextricably linked to climate — and these groups are also the most vulnerable to climate change. They will require far greater access to technologies, markets, information and credit for investment to adjust their production systems and practices to climate change.... [Climate change] will also affect food availability by reducing the productivity of crops, livestock and fisheries, and hinder access to food by disrupting the liveli-hoods of millions of rural people who depend on agriculture for their incomes. (FAO 2016b: v)

The policy framework is directed toward increasing the resource-use ef-ficiency of smallholders while reducing the fossil fuel use and environmental degradation as well as enhancing sustainable production and tapering off chemical input dependence. Indeed, according to the report, agricultural sectors should decouple emissions from production increases, with a specific focus on smallholder farm families and threats to their livelihoods posed by climate change: "Most of the world's poor and hungry are rural people who earn meagre livings from agriculture. In 2010, some 900 million of the estimated 1.2 billion extremely poor lived in rural areas. About 750 million of them worked in agriculture, usually as smallholder family farmers" (FAO 2016b: 46).

The main focus is on small farmers and innovation in farming systems: "innovation often builds on and adjusts local knowledge and traditional sys-tems, in combination with new sources of knowledge from formal research systems" (FAO 2016b: 50). This innovation is referred to in two contexts: in regard to local knowledge and traditional systems is agroecology, and in formal research systems are sustainable intensification and biotechnologies (low and high tech), which can also lead to innovative management practices. In this way, agroecology is described as the local and traditional basis of peasant farming, which involves working with nature and produces the highest proportion of the food in the world. Innovation should be incorporated in it.

This analytical framework was incorporated into an official FAO policy dialogue as an outcome of the biotech symposium. Following the agroecology process, the first global biotech symposium was supposed to follow the same format with regional dialogues and a final event summarizing the outcomes and sending recommendations for the different FAO committees. The first regional biotech symposium was planned to take place in Malaysia in September 2017. The IPC tried to facilitate the participation of CSOs in the symposium advisory panel and proposed some panellists for the event; however, this was not successful due to the lack of time given to consult and continuous changes in the process. It became evident that the symposium was being organized in such a way as to co-opt agroecology. Because the IPC had received a late invitation to join the symposium steering committee, other NGOs shared their notes from the first preparatory meeting, which made clear how Moore's vision regarding the failure of GMOs to increase yields was also shared by the promoters of the biotech symposium:

> Meantime we see innovation as an engine to drive economic developments to facilitate and enable especially family farmers to achieve the development goals is not necessarily turned on in many developing countries. So in other words, the engine of innovation has not played its role as it should have been. Biotechnology is one of these innovations. One of approaches. Biotechnology is continued to be developed but not in speed and scope as we hoped. We have seen over these years that lots of different ideas and debates come up, especially sort of polarized debate. Also focus on one hand, research, science and technology are been developed rapidly. But other hand in terms of application and adaption of these technologies and access to these technologies by smallholders and family farmers is very much lacking behind. Regulatory aspects in many countries still lacking. Also, another polarized situation is equaling biotechnologies with transgenic and GMOs. We see governments also confused whether or not they should promote the development and application of biotechnologies. As these could be perceived as promoting GMOs in certain countries. Or maybe perceived as promoting benefit of multinationals.

At the first regional biotech symposium in Malaysia, the IPC participated with a delegation of fifteen people. This small delegation raised concerns about all of the pro-GMO panel presentations, which contradicted a background document for the symposium outlining that the event would "focus on a broad range of agricultural biotechnologies, including many 'low-tech applications', for example fermentation processes, bio-fertilizers, artificial insemination, the production of vaccines, disease diagnostics, the development of biopesticides and the use of molecular markers in developing new varieties and breeds" (FAO 2017a: 2). Further, stated the document, "none of these involves the production of genetically modified organisms (or GMOs) and it is inaccurate to equate biotechnologies to GMOs only" (FAO 2017a: 2).

After various informal talks with the FAO officers in charge of the process, who tried to prevent the public expression of any opposing view in the plenary discussion, the IPC presented its concerns in a formal letter to the regional and central FAO offices. "The conference was biased towards agricultural biotechnologies, especially GMOs, from the very beginning," noted the letter. Only three CSOs were permitted among the more than forty presentations, "most of which spoke about lab research, with little mention of demonstrated socioeconomic and ecological impacts on smallholders. The moderation of most sessions was very limited in their encouragement of balanced discussions, especially suppressing genuine concerns of smallholders."

Unexpectedly, the symposia in Latin America and the Middle East were cancelled, after USAID (among the participants in the event in Malaysia) withdrew its support for the process. The same funding countries (the United States, the Netherlands, and Switzerland) decided to ask the same FAO officers to organize the final global symposium as a standalone event and, taking advantage of the United Nations Decade for Family Farming that started in 2019, they changed its name to the International Symposium on Agricultural Innovation for Family Farmers. It was no longer based on the outcomes of the regional biotech meetings.

The 2016 FAO biotech symposium was steered toward a deeper discussion of regulation of NBTs, which were endorsed by the International Seed Federation during its 2017 annual congress in Budapest, which gathered 1,680 delegates from sixty-eight countries. Jean-Christophe Gouache, president of the International Seed Federation, declared that the aim was to "re-emphasize the seed industry's commitment and contribution to finding solutions for an effective access and benefit sharing system as part of the International Treaty [on] Plant Genetic Resources" (*European Seed* 2017). The congress saw the launch of the World Seed Partnership, a joint effort by the OECD, International Seed Testing Association, International Union for the Protection of New Varieties of Plants, and International Seed Federation to support the development of the seed sector in countries worldwide to achieve internationally harmonized seed systems, a matter of urgency given current government discussions on regulatory frameworks for NBTs. "The fact is that regulatory policy will determine the methods used across companies and across crops. Policies that place an overly high regulatory burden on new plant breeding innovations will limit use to only the largest companies and only the highest value crops, such as corn and soybeans," states an article in the industry magazine *SeedWorld*. "While countries around the world chart new territories in determining how plant breeding innovations should be handled, the international seed industry hopes policymakers will create frameworks that give legal certainty to plant breeders and developers, foster innovation and ensure safety" (Deering 2017).

The World Seed Partnership seeks for governments to adopt a zero-regulation approach to gene-editing techniques (as presented in the side event of the FAO biotech symposium). Indeed, the International Seed Federation (2016: 4) developed the "consistent criteria for the scope of regulatory oversight," affirming as a central concept that "plant varieties developed through the latest breeding methods should not be differentially regulated if they are similar or indistinguishable from varieties that could have been produced through earlier breeding methods." In order to support this campaign, the International Seed Federation developed a toolkit on how to guide public discussion in order to present NBTs as a natural evolution in the history of agriculture and human selection of seeds.

The final part of the toolkit focuses on public policies and regulatory frameworks for NBTs with the objective of attaining a "consistent approach to determining which categories of products will not fall under current GMO regulations" so as to "provide plant breeders with legal certainty regarding access to innovation" (International Seed Federation 2017a: 8). It reaffirms the principle that governments should regulate plants developed under the latest breeding methods as no different from those produced through earlier breeding methods. So the ultimate goal is to present the NBTs as a natural process to find a loophole that will exclude them from current GMO regulations. This would allow for penetration of the European market and justify the lack of GMO labelling for consumers. It is interesting to note the evident role of global governance through public policies since they are crucial to reducing costs for corporations through homogenous regulation of NBTs. The International Seed Federation (2017a: 8) provides key messages under the headings of research and development ("plant breeders need a clear policy framework and predictability to enable a long-term approach to the investment in developing new varieties"), movement of seed and trade ("inconsistent policies and practices put plant breeders at a competitive disadvantage and make it more costly to get innovative products onto the market") and rules and regulations ("The cost of over-regulation means it takes longer to develop new varieties as pre-market assessments are needed before a new variety can enter the market").

In order to be effective at lobbying, the World Seed Partnership engaged a Brussels-based consultant to map the different actors participating in the discussion of the regulatory framework. The European market is a main target of the lobbying work, as exemplified by a case at the European Court of Justice. In December 2015, nine CSOs and peasant organizations stormed the French Council of State demanding a moratorium on the cultivation of varieties that have developed a tolerance of herbicides, which poison soils, water, and food. They also demanded the strict implementation of GMO regulations for NBTs. The Council of State decided to refer the matter to the European Court of Justice in October 2016, asking it to clarify the legal status of organisms that are the result of "classic" mutagenesis and new techniques of site-directed mutagenesis, such as CRISPR-Cas9. The Council of State also wanted to clarify whether European states have the right to regulate varieties resulting from mutagenesis that would not be classified under the European regulations on GMOs.

The European Court of Justice was thus asked to give a judgement, which the states and the European Commission would have to respect, regarding whether NBTs fell under the GMO Directive 2001/18/EC. At the same time, the European Commission made use of its Scientific Advice Mechanism to get a scientific opinion on new NBTs. In January 2018 the commission's lawyer argued that those techniques could not be exempted from GMO regulations due to safety concerns, but rather due to internal market issues. Finally, in July 2018, the European Court of Justice ruled that GMO regulations should apply to techniques such as CRISPR- Cas9. This debate was further bolstered by the Dutch government's proposal to modify Directive 2001/18/EC so plants resulting from NBTs could be exempt and released into the environment without any kind of monitoring. In contrast, opponents of NBTs argue that the techniques should follow the regulation, not the final product.

The IPC raised the issue of how NBTs could lead to the patenting of what are called native traits of genetic resources. Mapping a plant's genome al- lows researchers to identify genes of interest, and if they attach some new characteristics to a gene (e.g., resistance to floods) it can be considered an invention and be patented. After patenting, the intellectual property rights can be transferred to all local varieties and wild crop relatives worldwide. For instance, any plant containing the "natural" equivalent of the patented biological material can be patented according to Directive 98/44/EC:

> This framework does not protect a technique, a process, a biological material or any product. It allows patenting the genetic information, meaning a series of plants or animals very different [from] each other, that cannot be reduced to a single plant variety or one animal species: all might contain one similar genetic information and express a hereditary character or function associated with this specific genetic information — which stands for the resistance to an insect or herbicide, precocity, nutritional quality, taste, etc. So, varieties breeders and peasants will not be owners of those patents, but if they work or cultivate that plants, they will face great difficulties in demonstrating that they did not use the patented plants, but natural vegetables before the planned modification of the gene and patented. In this sense, they could be accused of theft and forgery. Within this patenting framework, seeds industries will have an exclusive monopoly for the commercial utilization of those seeds. (Mori and Onorati 2017)

The European Union adopted Directive 98/44/EC on the legal protection of biotechnological inventions in 1998. This directive essentially states that plant varieties and animal breeds, along with essentially biological processes to obtain plants or animals (such as breeding or selection), are not patentable. What is patentable according to the directive are (a) microbiological processes (a manipulation happening at the cell level, or genetic modification, is a microbiological process); (b) an isolated gene or one produced with a microbiological process, even if it is identical to a natural gene; (c) genetic material (the chemical material composing the gene); and (d) genetic information (digitized information on the composition of gene). Patents of biological material and genetic information also cover products that contain these biological materials (genes, proteins) or genetic information. At the time the directive was adopted, transgenic products were mainly covered. But the industry tried to find a way to also patent non-genetically-modified plants since society was rejecting GMOs. Given that the directive was written under the strong influence of industry, it contains several loopholes.

The first problem is that the directive does not say that a *product* resulting from an essentially biological process is not patentable. The directive just says that an essentially biological process is not patentable. This is why the industry has been looking for ways of patenting material that is not regulated as genetically modified. Initially, the industry tried to put a patent on native genes with a specific function that could be explained (e.g., tolerance to a herbicide, resistance to an insect). Even though this did not constitute an invention, the fact that the knowledge of the link between the gene and its function had not been made public before (through a patent, a catalogue, or a scientific publication) is what was considered new and allowed a company to patent it, regardless of whether the plant was bred through essentially biological processes. This is usually called a patent on a native trait. The European Commission published an interpretation on this issue, stating that the legislator, when writing the directive on patents, intended that products developed through an essentially biological process could not be patented. But the European Patent Office is still granting such patents.

The European Patent Office grants patents not only for countries in the European Union but also for other countries who have signed the European Patent Convention (around forty countries in total). Moreover, in Articles 8 and 9, Directive 98/44/EC states that the protection of a patent extends to all of the products that have the particular gene or genetic information and express its function, regardless of whether it is a patent on genetic material (the chemical material composing the gene) or genetic information (digitized information on the composition of the gene). In the past, transgenesis (insertion of genes from different species) was not a problem because it was easy to distinguish the transgenic material in the plant. But with new genetic engineering techniques, it is no longer easy to distinguish modified biological material or modified genetic information from a gene or genetic information already existing in a wild plant that stems exclusively from biological processes.

Both the patenting of genetic information and the opportunity to patent the native traits of seeds raise a strong question regarding data related to DSI, which generally refers to the information component of genetic resources, or of their parts and components. DSI can be acquired by technicians and may lead to the resynthesizing of genetic resources in a lab, making it unnecessary to physically access the genetic resource. DSI is not included in the ITPGRFA or any other instrument for access and benefit-sharing, which may well lead to commercial applications and the privatization of traditional seeds and related knowledge.

The ITPGRFA has a central role in this discussion, since it aims to establish a global system to provide farmers, plant breeders, and scientists with access to plant genetic materials. Parties to the treaty "agree to make their genetic diversity and related information about the crops stored in their gene banks available to all through the MLS [Multilateral System]" (FAO 2019b). The Multilateral System allows access to the world's gene banks, including the vast collections of the Consultative Group on International Agricultural Research, a consortium of fifteen international research centres. In 2017, during a meeting of the ITPGRFA's Governing Body, the issue of DSI was raised by the IPC through Guy Kastler of Vía Campesina, who requested the protection of these public resources by applying the same rules to both genetic information and genetic material:

> Open internet access to digital sequence information on PGRFAS [plant genetic resources for food and agriculture] shared by the Treaty's Global Information System could act in breach of either the treaty or the Convention on Biological Diversity.

> The digital sequence information found in each PGRFA could be considered as an integral part to the latter, and accessing such information is linked to benefit-sharing obligations and to the ban on claiming intellectual property rights, and indeed any other right that may limit access to the PGRFA, its genetic parts, or components. It is clear to us peasant farmers that living plants can only be considered as a whole.

> Some researchers and the industry, however, believe quite the opposite. They believe that digital sequence information is not linked to the PGRFA that it is found in. In this scenario, the Convention on Biological Diversity and the Declaration on Indigenous Peoples thus applies, and in particular the obligations regarding free, informed, prior consent and benefit-sharing. Digital sequence information that bears information on an associated function does not constitute a scientific creation once it has been patented. The information directly comes from the traditional knowledge of the farmers and Indigenous communities who have bred and conserved the PGRFAS that contain these sequences and describe their function.

> Against this background, the treaty should not disseminate such digital sequence information that comes from PGRFAS without restriction, until the following have been achieved: ensure that benefit-sharing is upheld, a ban is in place on claiming intellectual

property rights or any other rights that limit facilitated access to the PGRFAs found in the Multilateral System, their genetic parts, or genetic components.

The issue was so central that it was reiterated in the final declaration made by TAMs for food sovereignty, which asked the parties to the treaty to protect the genetic material held in Consultative Group on International Agricultural Research centres from the risk of dematerialization, which is leading to the patenting of traits of in-trust material. The IPC requested that the treaty parties "act urgently before more patents on native traits fall under the control of an ever-smaller number of multinational seed companies that would privatize all PGRFA [plant genetic resources for food and agriculture] essential for food security, and thus control the entire food chain." The IPC also took the chance to lobby the European Union and asked the European Commission for a new interpretation of Directive 98/44/EC, saying that the scope of a patent cannot be extended to biological material or genetic information that can be produced through essentially biological processes, even if it has been obtained through new patentable genetic modification techniques. Kastler stated:

> The European Union said that access to digital sequence information is not linked to access to physical resources. This is not what Article 9 of its own 1998 Directive on the protection of biotechnological inventions (98/44/EC) says: "The protection conferred by a patent on a product containing or consisting of genetic information shall extend to all material, save as provided in Article 5(1), in which the product in incorporated and in which the genetic information is contained and performs its function." According to the European Union, digital sequence information would be independent of biological material when it comes to access, but would no longer be so when it comes to patents on genetic information that allow claim rights to biological material. These patents infringe plant breeders' rights to free access to relevant PGRFA [plant genetic resources for food and agriculture] for research and breeding, and the rights of farmers to cultivate and trade them. They are therefore not in line with the commitments of the contracting parties that have approved the treaty's Material Transfer Agreement, and in particular Article 6.2, which prohibits the beneficiary of access to plant genetic resources of the Multilateral System from claiming a right to intellectual property

that would limit facilitated access to the material provided, its parts, or genetic components, within which the patented genetic information has been identified.

Industry is on the verge of success in patenting native traits of existing plant varieties through use of NBTs, and the patenting of genetic information will allow the appropriation of biodiversity and peasant farming. At the meeting of ITPGRFA's Governing Body, the IPC explained its concerns to the attending governments, especially those of Latin America, for whom the IPC provided interpretation services during the evening sessions. (The governments from the Global North usually choose to discuss the most contentious issues during the evening sessions, as they have larger delegations to cover the different schedules, unlike smaller delegations with one or two representatives who cannot attend all events. Further, evening sessions sometimes lack interpreters and thus negotiations proceed in English.) National patent legislation cannot allow the patenting of plants or animals that result exclusively from essentially biological processes, including the elements that constitute them and the genetic information they carry.

The seed industry wants to reform the International Convention for the Protection of New Varieties of Plants, which lays the foundation for the work of the International Union for the Protection of New Varieties of Plants. This project will suppress for five years (after the acquisition of the breeders' rights) the "breeder's exemption," which allows the use of a protected variety to breed another one. The industry also wants to replace the current description of a variety (based on the physical traits of the plants from which the variety originates) with dematerialized genetic information (International Union for the Protection of New Varieties of Plants 2021). This information would include easily identifiable genetic markers, enabling industry to identify a particular variety, or even a new variety coming from a cross with a protected variety, in farm fields, in produce, and in processed products. The physical traits that are currently used for identification can only be determined on a farmer's field by sending in a group of experts, and this method only generates a small amount of royalties. Thanks to the traceability of genetic markers, the new plant breeders' rights would become as efficient as the current patents in detecting fraud in silos and ships transporting grain, or in flour, or in shops' inventories. But, as opposed to the current patents, they would offer the advantage — for the seed producer who seeks to hide their GMOs — of not requiring a description of the breeding process.

The Netherlands held the presidency of the Europe Council for the first half of 2016 and announced the intention of putting on the agenda the question of whether products created through NBTs should be considered GMOs or GMO-free and whether patents should be permitted on the native traits of plants facilitated by these new techniques. The Netherlands opposes patents on plants and plant traits and believes that if patents are still permitted, there should at least be a complete breeder's exemption. Thus, traceability is still a crucial issue to be discussed since it confronts toxicity and any GMO-related problems for humans, animals, and the environment. In addition, the IPC requested traceability in order to differentiate products from patented inventions and thus prevent the extension of patent protection to native traits. Yet, without traceability, there is no patent.

For its part, the WFO supports the introduction of NBTs using the narrative of climate change — that is, supporting a decrease in chemical and nutritional inputs, and thus reducing the impact of agriculture on the environment, improving production efficiency, and increasing food safety. According to the WFO, NBTs will allow farmers access to new varieties in a shorter time frame than traditional breeding does. However, in reality, the WFO's position on NBTs is expressed by its European component Copa-Cogeca, with Copa representing farmers and Cogeca representing farmers' cooperatives. The main issue for the WFO and Copa-Cogeca has to do with the patenting of non–essentially biological processes.

"Patent law is an inappropriate instrument for the EU agriculture sector. All genetic resources must remain readily available for farmers and breeders so that they can make progress in the breeding sector," according to Thor Kofoed, chair of the Copa-Cogeca Seeds Working Party (Agripress 2016). Copa-Cogeca Secretary-General Pekka Pesonen noted that the European Commission's recommendation against patenting products created through essentially biological processes did not clearly address NBTs and natural traits achieved through non–essentially biological processes. "Moreover, the Commission's recommendation is not legally binding and the EPO [European Patent Office] is an independent body," he said, calling on "national governments to ensure that the EPO respects the Commission's recommendation in order to ensure that existing plants do not fall under the scope of patent law" (Agripress 2016). Although the WFO and Copa-Cogeca have raised the issue of patenting essentially biological processes, they also consider NBTs a matter of urgency since they are defending and representing the interests of commercial farmers and aiming to maximize profits from agriculture. Certain WFO member have expressed concerns, such as Coldiretti (Italy) and COAG (Spain), which oppose the adoption of NBTs, mainly because they can be used to appropriate the basic resources of the organic sector through patenting. The only concern voiced directly by the WFO at an international level has to do with the application of NBTs to livestock, which is also a matter related to sector concentration due to the high level of investments in technology in the sector.

The integration of family farming in the global value chain is hindered by limits on the concentration of the agricultural sector, mainly in Europe, where TNCs are in direct competition with family farmers. So on the one side, the WFO supports NBTs as a way forward to increase the productivity and profitability of farming (with some safeguards for the organic sector), but on the other side the WFO does not take into consideration the concentration process needed to develop NBTs, which is seen in the current trend of mergers and acquisitions in the agricultural sector.

Another relevant actor in regards to seeds and agricultural biodiversity is IFOAM. In general, IFOAM participates in the FAO at a technical level in regard to normative processes and to a lesser extent in CSO processes, probably due to the mixed nature of its constituency, whereby it does not have only food producers in its membership. Its only relevant participation at the European level has been in the Regional Symposium on Agroecology for Europe in 2016. The organization's main aim is to have products derived from NBTs accurately classified and regulated — that is, assessed not on the basis of the product but the process — in order to avoid their penetration into the organic sector. IFOAM determined in 1993 that organic farming could not include the use of GMOs, and in 1999 the European Union regulation on organic farming disallowed the use of GMOs in the production process. This regulation has been considered a benchmark for all private organic standards and governments who prohibit the use of GMOs in organic production at any stage of the value chain. Due to the increasing attention being paid to NBTs, IFOAM (2017) released a position paper reaffirming the principles of organic agriculture (health, ecology, fairness, and care) to be applied when evaluating all of the new techniques used in creating genotypes.

IFOAM seeks to make the disclosure of breeding techniques in organic production mandatory, which would involve public authorities guaranteeing transparency and guaranteeing consumers the freedom to make an informed decision. At the same time, it is clear that the patenting of native traits or traits deriving from traditional breeding (for both older and newly bred varieties) should not be permitted. The organic sector that IFOAM represents includes both peasant farming and commercial farming, with no specificity regarding the role of labour. In the markets, IFOAM has elaborated innovative solutions, mostly working on short circuits and local markets, and connecting consumers and producers through Participatory Guarantee Systems. In this sense, markets are separated from capitalism as in the model of Arrighi.

However, no opposition to capitalist accumulation is expressed, considering that TNCs are investing in organic certified production.

Thus, the global governance of agriculture is witnessing an intensification of conflicts. This clash between intellectual property rights and collective rights at this moment is focused on agriculture biodiversity as well the Convention on Biological Diversity and ITPGRFA, where negotiations should try to harmonize different aspects of the FAO policy frameworks on climate change. The transnational policy space shown in Figure 3.1 should be revised along these lines, with less space for the WTO and TRIPS. Since the failure of the 2003 WTO negotiations in Cancun, international trade has moved forward through bilateral free trade agreements (with a similar fragmentation observed in the GATT), while the space for governing biodiversity has become more complex with new technological developments and growing relationships between the different international bodies.

In April 2018 the FAO (n.d.b) held the Second International Symposium on Agroecology with more than six hundred participants from governments, international NGOs, TAMs, and private companies, to "synthesize and build on the outcomes of the regional meetings, and provide an opportunity to share and discuss policies that can help scale-up and scale-out agroecology in order to achieve the Sustainable Development Goals." The symposium was also an opportunity to shift the dialogue from a technical to a political one, with pressure put on FAO Director-General Graziano da Silva (almost at the end of his term) to leave a clear legacy in the FAO's Strategic Programmes and Regional Initiatives. The final outcome of the symposium should have been sent to the next FAO Committee on Agriculture for endorsement and then to the FAO Conference. The first proposal from the director-general was to have a final declaration agreed upon in the plenary by all of the governments and the different participants. However, after a first meeting of the drafting team with a small group of governments, FAO officers, civil society as represented by the IPC (in this case Vía Campesina and another TAM called MAELA took charge), and some experts, it became clear that the governments would not come to an agreement among themselves and other stakeholders. So the declaration was just presented as the chair's summary (FAO 2018a). The IPC managed to have some problematic wording, such as "taking advantage of new opportunities for digitalisation, communications, and networking based on open-source software," removed for the final document. At the same time, the Second International Symposium on Agroecology received the FAO proposal to follow up the work through a Scaling Up Agroecology Initiative and agreed on a definition of agroecology for the FAO based on ten common interlinked and interdependent characteristics of agroecological systems (see Figure 4.1).

In October 2018 the FAO's Committee on Agriculture met to decide upon the Scaling Up Agroecology Initiative as well as support for the ten elements of agroecology to guide to the transition to sustainable agriculture and food systems. The Committee on Agriculture endorsed the ten elements, but the North American region, with the support of the Netherlands, asked the FAO "to further revise them to reflect the discussions of this session" (FAO 2019a: 4). The explicit request coming from the floor during the plenary was to weave innovation among the principles, with reference to the outcomes of the upcoming Innovation for Family Farmers symposium, to be sent to the FAO Council. So the Innovation for Family Farmers symposium, held in Rome in November 2018, played a central role in supporting the incorporation of NBTs into agroecology through the inclusion of the innovation principle. The preparation process was again quite problematic for CSOs, and the officer in charge feared a similar result to the biotech symposium held in Asia in 2017. The IPC worked through its informal contacts with governments and FAO officers to understand how the same difficult process for the symposium was being used again. Despite wide participation (about six hundred participants) in the Innovation for Family Farmers symposium, there was no vibrant discussion at the end and the final outcome, which was presented as a chair's summary (FAO 2018c), was contested by the delegations of Iran, the Netherlands, and Switzerland due to the lack of recommendations about innovation. The U.S. delegation intervened to defend the chair's summary, exposing a division in the bloc of governments. Civil society, led by the IPC, played a rather active role intervening from the floor, pointing out the unequal participation of family farmers on the panels and aiming to protect the outcomes of the four-year-long FAO agroecology process from the result of a standalone event.

In the same week, the Fourteenth Conference of Parties of the Convention on Biological Diversity met in Sharm El Sheikh, Egypt, with a clear agenda point on DSI. Governments delayed the discussion to avoid regulation of DSI, which the IPC delegation condemned given its importance:

> By reducing the genetic modifications thus obtained to a simple dematerialized "information" to fit into computer algorithms, the industry extends the scope of its patents to all plants, animals or microorganisms that naturally contain the same "information." The patent on the genetic information associated with genes that accelerate the growth of chickens thus allows the appropriation of all naturally fast-growing chickens! We had hoped that this genetic information would be verified so that we could ban these patents

Figure 4.1 Ten Elements of Agroecology

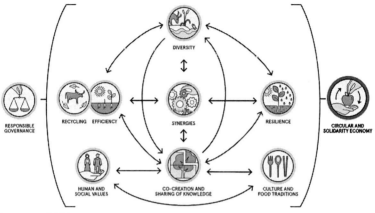

Source: FAO (2018b)

on "native genes." (Vía Campesina 2018)

During the negotiations, the IPC asked for the use of DSI to be regulated according to the Nagoya Protocol on Access and Benefit-Sharing, so that free, prior, and informed consent would be implemented regarding access to material genetic resources and digital information. It noted that "open access" should not mean a lack of regulations and that those seeking access "must clearly state what is the final objective of the use of this information." Further, "due to the fact that information is useful for scientific research and for the conservation of genetic resources, digital information cannot be used for economic purposes, and for this reason cannot be used to patent new genetic resources that are generated by this information."

The conflict is still ongoing. The coordinated intervention of the new TAMs for food sovereignty in two parallel fora was a first step to scale up their organization in the space of transnational governance of agriculture, which was discussed and agreed upon at the IPC General Meeting in 2018 in Cape Town. Twenty-two years after the 1996 NGO Forum, which identified the FAO as an entry point to confront the financialization of agriculture, the IPC took up the strategy using its consolidated position in the FAO to intervene at the international level using an institutional guerrilla approach.

5 Conclusion

In this book, I have read the policy negotiations of TAMs in the space of global governance of agriculture in the broader framework of cycles of capital accumulation, with a specific focus on the inclusion of NBTs and DSI in agroecology, which would allow the appropriation of the world's biodiversity and the full transition of peasant agriculture to capital accumulation circuits. The starting point for the analysis was the latest developments of the strategy of radical TAMs supporting food sovereignty in the specific space of global governance of agriculture. Assuming a theoretical framework composed of three tiers (Arrighi and Moore's world-systems theory, Edelman and Borras's international critical agrarian studies, and Coleman's nonterritorial governance), I presented the progressive achievements of radical TAMs in the FAO — such as the *Right to Food Guidelines, Voluntary Guidelines on Tenure, Voluntary Guidelines for Securing Sustainable Small-Scale Fisheries,* Committee on World Food Security reform, International Year of Family Farming, and agroecology — as part of a counterhegemonic strategy to confront neoliberal policies in agriculture.

This strategy reached an important milestone during FAO Director-General Graziano da Silva's mandate. The symposia on agroecology (2014–18) recognized agroecology and family farming as central to rural development and tackling climate change. However, corporate powers have been trying to include NBTs and DSI in agroecology, presenting them as a solution to make family farmers more resilient to climate change. This book reads the introduction of NBTs and DSI as an attempt to expand the external agroecological frontier and to create the conditions for a new phase of accumulation based on the appropriation of nature. Lowering the cost of food production through dispossession and shifting capital accumulation to a new phase of material expansion (Moore 2010c; Smith 2007) would result in increasing the yields of agricultural production and overcoming the superweed effect.

At the same time, at the global governance level, NBTs and DSI are key processes in trying to resolve the dichotomy of the global governance of agriculture, which was defined at the beginning of the 1990s with the emergence of two normative frameworks: the WTO's TRIPS Agreement and the Rio Conventions and their promotion of collective rights. The inclusion of NBTs and DSI in the agroecology framework is at the core of the ongoing confrontation between TAMs and corporate powers struggling for a new material expansion of the economy based on different models of agriculture. The former is moving toward the realization of food sovereignty through agroecology, and the second aims to complete the transition of peasant agriculture into capitalism (Edelman and Borras 2016).

The introduction of NBTs and DSI could allow the patenting of biodiversity without the production of new varieties, capturing into the capital accumulation the current peasant varieties and wild crop relatives that are supplying raw materials. Borrowing from the concept of cognitive biocapitalism (Fumagalli and Lucarelli 2011), DSI can be explained as intellectual property rights being used to appropriate a general intellect into codified knowledge. This has instigated a new phase of material expansion through accumulation by dispossession (or appropriation), intensifying the proletarianization and class differentiation of the peasantry, still persisting in the fields through the Chayanovian model of peasant agriculture.

On the other side, the full implementation of biodiversity conservation policies, such as the Convention on Biological Diversity, the Nagoya Protocol, and the ITPGRFA, through the policy framework derived from agroecology and family farming would overcome the dichotomy in the global governance of agriculture in favour of sustainable agriculture and collective rights to access natural resources, including information incorporated in genetic resources and held in the Consultative Group on International Agricultural Research databases and gene banks. This could lead to a new possible material and commercial expansion based on agroecology and repeasantization of the model of agriculture and development, which public policies (Copeland 2019) and private investments should support, as agroecology and family farming would play a central role in addressing climate change.

After the end of the Bretton Woods agreements, the financialization of agriculture restructured both the countryside and the space of global governance of agriculture. Out of this process emerged the new TAMs supporting the food sovereignty agenda, which contributed to reshaping the global governance of agriculture itself as a contested space with neoliberal policies. Indeed, the financialization of agriculture generated a dichotomous global governance space, in which TAMs established a new political take on food sovereignty, resisting any further penetration of capital into agriculture from within the production process, by engaging in policy dialogue with governments rather than by taking state power. In the dichotomous space of global governance, the financialization of agriculture, as part of the general financialization process, is driving capital penetration in the countryside and creating the conditions for a new material expansion through the appropriation of the world's biodiversity. This appropriation of biodiversity would intensify capital penetration in the internal agroecological frontier while expanding the external frontier to include all of the biodiversity in the capital accumulation system. A sort of class differentiation has occurred among the TAMs with the arrival of the food sovereignty movement, which is trying to oppose the financialization phase, fostering a new material expansion based on agroecology and the repeasantization of the mode of production, which compensates labour and natural resources rather than capital.

The drop in profit rates that caused the end of Bretton Woods was due to a crisis of overaccumulation and underproduction (too few raw materials), as the rate of profit is inversely proportional to the value of the raw materials (Marx 1967 III: 119). Paradoxically, it was the end of the Bretton Woods agreements that gave new centrality to the Bretton Woods institutions, the IMF and World Bank, via structural adjustment policies, which imposed macroeconomic stabilization policies based on privatization, free market development, and agro-exports in the 1980s and 1990s. The new neoliberal policy framework of austerity, economic structural adjustment programs, and bilateral and multilateral trade agreements led to the Uruguay Round of GATT negotiations from 1986 to 1994, which culminated in the formation of the WTO in 1995. These institutions, together with the United Nations, gained a central role in global governance.

Neoliberal economic policies, deregulation, and the liberalization of global markets have characterized the financialization of the economy, which in this book was defined in relation to the mode of capital accumulation and not in relation to actors (e.g., financial institutions or the corporate sector) being more active in the economy. Thus, financialization means capital accumulation proceeding through financial deals according to the M-M′ formula, with capital being free from its commodity form. Accumulation through financial deals means the absence of a trickle-down effect to the workers in the accumulation process, resulting in an increasing social polarization and class differentiation process, with a disappearing middle class as well as rising competition for money capital between nation-states and enterprises.

Beyond the main narrative, which portrays financialization as destabilizing the economy, we saw that financialization emerges from a fall in profit rates and has a stabilizing effect on the economic cycle, guaranteeing the continuity of capital accumulation. The increasing competition leads to growing vertical and horizontal integration among enterprises, pushing toward new organizational processes, in order to reestablish profitability. Indeed, research into new financial arenas for portfolio differentiation and new modes of organization of production allows capital to seep into agriculture, on the one hand creating new markets (as in the financialization of nature), but on the other hand creating the conditions for an organizational revolution. If capital penetration into the countryside does not foster agricultural innovation, the accumulation regime will shift to a financialization phase in order to maintain profits, and will revert back to the countryside as an agrifinancialization process, which operates through accumulation by dispossession, intensifying the proletarianization and class differentiation of the peasantry, in order to finally spur an organizational revolution reestablishing profitability and restarting the material cycle of expansion.

This organizational revolution did not happen with GMOs due to their commercial ban and failure to increase productivity, so the current agrifinancialization process is targeting NBTs and DSI to allow the complete penetration of capital into peasant agriculture, appropriating the world's biodiversity through the patenting of native traits, which are the foundation of the peasant mode of production. This appropriation is allowing a new ecological surplus through the expansion of the agroecological frontier, allowing the capitalist cycle of accumulation to include resources that were previously outside of the frontier. This process does not require the material seeds; thanks to DSI, it is similar to the commodity futures market, which involves a virtual process driving the real one. As we saw, this organizational revolution in agriculture could follow different paths, such as the agroecological one promoted by the new TAMs as a framework for agricultural policies in the United Nations milieu, especially in the FAO. In the case that the agroecology framework prevails, the material expansion will start again without compensating the invested capital, but rather compensating the labour of a labour-intensive model of production.

The result is that capital accumulation and TAMs are confronting one another in the space of transnational governance of agriculture, trying to define the policies supporting a new organizational revolution in agriculture to move toward a new phase of material expansion. Indeed, the tensions and conflicting currents in the transnational governance of agriculture are increasing and fragmenting the space itself, to the point that it is impossible to find a hegemonic state or actor that is able to create some coherence in governance at the moment. Bernstein (2010) noticed how in Marxism the class struggle was oriented toward the takeover of state power, but this aspect is absent from the TAMs' agenda. TAMs emerged as an autonomous network disconnected from traditional political parties, aiming to support local struggles through advocacy at the global level.

In this case, the definition of everyday politics and resistance in rural areas helps to clarify why TAMs and the food sovereignty movement do not seek to take over the central or local government. TAMs are building a different type of struggle from within the model of production through diverse forms of everyday politics (Scott and Kerkvliet 1986; Visser et al. 2015), not aiming to conquer institutional political power but rather to influence the political agenda by rewriting policy and normative frameworks at different levels (e.g., United Nations, national governments, and local authorities). TAMs use the negotiating power they derive from their base on the ground, which can adopt and implement or block the policies negotiated and approved at the different levels. In order to have an effective policy implementation process, the involvement of the most affected actors on the ground is necessary; otherwise, the everyday resistance practices in the model of production (controlled by the actors) can make the policy defined at the institutional level ineffective. This also explains the United Nation' civil society partnerships, which provide the opportunity to elevate resistance practices to the policy framework, but also present the risk of grassroots practices being co-opted into the industrial model of production and global value chains.

Class analysis is applied in an unorthodox way to the emergence of the TAMs for food sovereignty. The class differentiation from other TAMs is due to the further capital penetration into the countryside in the financialization phase. If we assume a perspective that is broader than transnational governance in agriculture, the new TAMs for food sovereignty are part of what Evans (2008: 271) calls counterhegemonic globalization, which he defines as "a globally organized project of transformation aimed at replacing the dominant (hegemonic) global regime with one that maximizes democratic political control and makes the equitable development of human capabilities and environmental stewardship its priorities." Arrighi and Silver (1999: 11) too, in the world-systems theory perspective, recognize the necessity of a political subjectivity acting at the transnational level:

> Formally democratic governments in much of the world are likely
> to make key economic and social policy decisions with "an eye

at least as much on pleasing the International Monetary Fund as appealing to an electorate." For Markoff, "the challenge of recreating democracy in the emerging world of transnational decision-making" can only be met by the organization of transnational democratic movements capable of extracting "concessions from the new holders of transnational power" (Markoff, 1996, 132–35).

Arrighi and Silver (1999: 282) also foresaw the emergence of social conflict during the financialization phase and the consequent proletarization process, which gave an emerging role to social movements beyond the dimension of class to include the worldwide dynamics of capitalism and colonialism:

> The disempowerment of social movements — the labor movement in particular — that has accompanied the global financial expansion of the 1980s and 1990s is largely a conjectural phenomenon. It signals the difficulties involved in delivering on the promises of the U.S.-sponsored global New Deal. A new wave of social conflict is likely, and can be expected to reflect the greater proletarianization, increasing feminization, and changing the spatial and ethnic configuration of the world's labor forces.

This structured social resistance influenced capitalist development, since the two main forms of antisystemic movements (class based and ethnic/nation based) reached the medium-term objective of attaining state power but failed in their long-term objective of ending class and ethnic oppression, giving space to new movements that — without the aim of attaining state power — contributed to the systemic crisis of the 1970s. At the same time, Arrighi Hopkins, and Wallerstein (1992) recognize the difficulty of finding a new ideology and set of strategies to foster social transformation. The outcome of this process of social transformation will depend on the dynamics of the social conflicts (this is relevant at the global level, not at the local or national one) emerging from the systemic chaos of the financialization phase: "The dilemmas of the antisystemic movements seem to be even more profound than those of the dominant forces of the world-system. In any case, without a strategy, there is no good reason to believe there is any invisible hand that will guarantee transformation in a good direction, even when and if the capitalist world-economy falls apart" (Arrighi, Hopkins, and Wallerstein 1992: 242).

In particular, following the peasants' wars (Wolf 1973), the peasantry was identified as a revolutionary force that influenced global power during the twentieth century. "The widespread current tendency to dismiss the working class as an important social force may be as premature as late nineteenth and early twentieth century dismissals of the peasantry as a revolutionary force," write Arrighi and Silver (1999: 216). "For just as peasant rebellions from China to Vietnam were fundamental to the formation and crisis of U.S. hegemony, so workers' rebellions in the same region of the world may turn out to be: fundamental to an understanding of the social origins of world hegemony in the twenty-first century. But just as the twentieth-century peasant rebellions were enmeshed in a broader revolt against the West, so we can expect future class conflict to be enmeshed in the changing balance of power between the Western and non-Western worlds."

In this analysis of the role of TAMs as a form of peasant agency with a specific function in the post–Bretton Woods space of global governance, it is important to observe their relationship with national governments in the space of transnational governance — in what Arrighi (quoting Gramsci) identifies as a passive revolution in which the struggle for renewal was led by a state rather than a class:

> The function of Piedmont in the Italian Risorgimento is that of a "ruling class." In reality, what was involved was not that throughout the peninsula there existed nuclei of a homogeneous ruling class whose irresistible tendency to unite determined the formation of the new Italian national State. These nuclei existed, indubitably, but their tendency to unite was extremely problematic; also, more importantly, they ... were not "leading".... They ... wanted a new force, independent of every compromise and condition, to become the arbiter of the Nation: this force was Piedmont.... Thus Piedmont had a function which can from certain aspects, be compared to that of a party, i.e. of the leading personnel of a social group (and in fact people always spoke of the "Piedmont party"): with the additional feature that it was in fact, a State, with an army, a diplomatic service, etc. (Gramsci 1971 in Arrighi 2003: 7)

Gramsci applies this function of a passive revolution, which consists of a revolutionary restoration to different states, including Serbia and France. Arrighi extends the passive revolution (a restoration-revolution comparable to a repression-accommodation) to all of the hegemonic passages of world capitalism, with the hegemonic state exercising a Piedmontese function in respect to the world-system.

In the current phase, despite the crisis and squeezing of the functions of the nation-state, Arrighi (1996) individuates the East Asia region, and

China in particular, as a possible state-region leading the hegemonic passage. And in fact, the Chinese candidate for the position of FAO director-general position, Qu Dongyu, was voted into office in 2019. It is worth noting that Moore (2012: 244–52) has cast doubt on China's ability to lead a new commercial expansion based on agricultural productivity:

> Worldwide, agricultural labor productivity ticked upwards slowly after 1990, rising to just 1.36% through 2005, over the 1.12% average of 1961–90 (Alston, Babcock & Pardey, 2010: 461). The modest increase was largely attributable to Chinese agricultural reform, which has yet to provide a kind of hegemonic model for the world-system along the lines of the Dutch, British, and American agricultures in their golden ages. Indeed, for all the remarkable accomplishments of the Chinese "miracle," labor productivity in industry and agriculture both remain one-quarter (or less) the average obtaining within the Global North (Jefferson, Hub & Su, 2006; Jin, Huang & Rozelle, 2010). There are few signs that China's ascent, however successful on its own terms, offers the kind of hegemonic model for industry and agriculture that might be emulated by our era's rising powers....
>
> China does not appear poised to launch an agricultural revolution of the sort we have known in the history of capitalism — one that not only feeds the ascendant power, but *leads* the system to a new expansion.

In this case, the counterhegemonic role of TAMs is pertinent. TAMs have no official membership in China but can still play a role in countries outside of China, as well as in the United Nations and other global governance spaces.

In conclusion, TAMs can be an object of analysis, along with the way new TAMs have emerged through a differentiation process in relation to the financialization that shapes agricultural policies at the grassroots and transnational levels. The squeeze of nation-state powers and the definition of a global space for transnational governance of agriculture, shaped in a dichotomous tension, has generated the emergence of new TAMs supporting food sovereignty. In supporting human rights and collective rights approaches, these new TAMs are in opposition to the WTO and intellectual property rights. They struggle from within the production process rather than try to take state power.

The methodological implications of the research are related to the use of observant participation and the impossibility of separating myself from the object of research. Undertaking this research would not have been possible if I were not embedded in the political struggle to change food policies. I derived most of the analysis and access to data and unofficial information from being part of the process. Now that the TAMs' strategy is shifting and the food sovereignty struggle is no longer centred on the Rome process, future investigations will require a greater number of researchers or the direct commitment of TAMs within the scholar-activist paradigm. For this study, it was enough to distinguish the position of the researcher as situated and part of the process, while still keeping a strong intellectual rigour, which can be traced back to the arguments provided.

The theoretical implications concern the distinct lens of analysis that I built, bridging critical agrarian studies and the world-systems theory of Arrighi (and its interpretation from Moore's perspective) in order to examine the new political space of transnational governance of agriculture and the emerging TAMs in the broader framework of capital accumulation. In this framework, the class analysis is not strictly applicable; however, the discussion has to deal with an external and internal side of capitalist agriculture. The study confirmed the relevance of TAMs as a form of peasant agency that has been able to combat the agrifinancialization process since the early 1990s and the WTO and Rio negotiations, through to the most recent discussions on family farming and the governance of biodiversity.

This is also relevant for the theories and groups that are neglecting the usefulness of struggling in the transnational space of governance, as Harvey (2003: 175–79) wrote:

> Hostility between the two trains of thought and style of organizing is already much in evidence within the anti-globalization movement. A whole wing of it sees the struggle to command the state apparatus as not only irrelevant but an illusory diversion. The answer lies, they say, in localization of everything....

> Some way must be found, both theoretically and politically, to move beyond the amorphous concept of "the multitude" without falling into the trap of "my community, locality, or social group right or wrong." Above all, the connectivity between struggles within expanded reproduction and against accumulation by dispossession must assiduously be cultivated.

From a theoretical point of view, the Arrighian approach to agrarian political economy opens up the possibility to further develop the analysis of this connection of struggles among three different layers: (a) cycles of accumulation, including the "anti-market" where capitalists and political powers meet; (b) market economy, related to the circulation phase, where dependency and world-systems theory focus on the centre-periphery polarization of production; and (c) the material life-labour-capital relations at the level of production. The traditional class differentiation discussion (Lenin 1964) relates to this lower layer, which is focused on the local dynamics and does not affect the top layer of capital accumulation, which is not based on the internal social dynamics of a nation-state (Arrighi and Piselli 2017). In this sense, the study contributes to connecting the social and global struggles and their relations with institutions and global market forces using the TAMs as a relevant agent acting in this connection. The research on the Gramscian framework of passive revolution offers a field through which to further investigate how "'relations within society' (involving the development of productive forces ...) that constitute the 'hegemonic systems within the state,' were inextricably linked to 'relations between international forces' ... that constitute 'the combination of states in hegemonic systems'" (Gramsci 1971 in Morton 2007: 69).

The policy implications indicate the possible overcoming of the dichotomy in the global governance of agriculture and resolution of the opposition between the regulation of intellectual property rights and collective rights, including the full implementation of the Convention on Biological Diversity, Nagoya Protocol, ITPGRFA, and all the other agreements. The political activism implications concern strategizing in the broader framework of capital accumulation to understand the roots of current policies and execute a strategic mapping of the space of transnational governance of agriculture, while taking into consideration how to develop institutional guerrilla warfare in the different institutional arenas, the dichotomy and internal fragmentation of this space, and the lack of coherence among some actors, including the different government delegations. Furthermore, this strategic mapping should include not only the spaces beyond the Rome process but also the regional and national spaces in order to be more effective at policy change. An additional level is the connection of horizontal struggles and practices of alternative systems, so as to coordinate and organize the everyday resistance in the fields. This approach is emerging in some regions, where the regional organizations are able to bring the political struggle to the intermediate Arrighian layer of economic and market organization.

References

African Center for Biodiversity. 2017. "The Three Agricultural Input Mega-Mergers: Grim Reapers of South Africa's Food and Farming Systems." acbio.org.za/wp-content/uploads/2022/04/Mega-Mergers-Summary-Bayer-Monsanto.pdf.

Agripress. 2016. "Not Allow Patents on Products Created via Essentially Biological Processes." November 26. agripressworld.com/start/artikel/581085/en.

Altieri, M., and C. Nicholls. 2020. "Agroecology and the Emergence of a Post COVID-19 Agriculture." *Agriculture and Human Values* 37.

Arrighi, G. 1994. *The Long Twentieth Century: Money, Power and the Origins of Our Times.* London: Verso.

____. 1996. "The Rise of East Asia: World Systemic and Regional Aspects." *International Journal of Sociology and Social Policy* 16, 7.

____. 2003. "Hegemony and Antisystemic Movements." Paper prepared for the International Seminar REGGEN 2003, Hegemony and Counterhegemony: Globalization Constraints and Regionalization Processes, Rio de Janeiro, August 2003. citeseerx.ist.psu.edu/document?repid=rep1&type=pdf&doi=1ba3b17fa7f9edd48eae27e8f897e0a29b20c808.

____. 2007. *Adam Smith in Bejing.* London: Verso.

Arrighi, G., T.K. Hopkins, and I. Wallerstein. 1992. "1989, the Continuation of 1968." *Review (Fernand Braudel Center)* 15, 2 (Spring).

Arrighi, G., and F. Piselli. 2017. "Il capitalismo in un contesto ostile. Faide, lotta di classe, migrazioni nella calabria tra otto e novecento." Rome: Donzelli.

Arrighi, G., and B.J. Silver. 1999. *Chaos and Governance in the Modern World System.* Minneapolis: University of Minnesota Press.

Baran, P., and P. Sweezy. 1966. *Monopoly Capital: An Essay on the American Economic and Social Order.* New York: Monthly Review Press.

Benbrook, C.M. 2012. "Impacts of Genetically Engineered Crops on Pesticide Use in the U.S. — The First Sixteen Years." *Environmental Sciences Europe* 24, 24.

Bernstein, H. 2006. "Is There an Agrarian Question in the 21st Century?" *Canadian Journal of Development Studies* 27, 4.

____. 2010. *Class Dynamics of Agrarian Change.* Halifax, NS, and Sterling, VA: Fernwood Publishing and Kumarian Press.

Borras, S.M., Jr. 2016. "Land Politics, Agrarian Movements and Scholar-Activism." academia.edu/41907724/Borras_inaugural_lecture_14_april_2016_final_formatted_pdf_for_printing.

Borras, S.M., Jr., and J. Franco. 2009. "TAMs Struggling for Land and Citizenship

Rights." IDS Working Paper 323.

Borras, S.M., Jr., J. Franco, S. Gómez, C. Kay, and M. Spoor. 2012. "Land Grabbing in Latin America and the Caribbean." *Journal of Peasant Studies* 39, 3–4.

Borras, S.M., Jr., J. Franco, R. Isakson, L. Levidow, and P. Vervest. 2016. "The Rise of Flex Crops and Commodities: Implications for Research." *Journal of Peasant Studies* 43, 1.

Braga, J.C. 2013. "Qual conceito de financeirizaçao compreende o capitalism contemporâneo?" In *A grande crise capitalista 2007–2013: gênese, conexões e tendências*, edited by A.S. Barroso and R. Souza. Sao Paulo: Fundação Maurício Grabois.

Braudel, F. 1972. *The Mediterranean and the Mediterranean World in the Age of Philip II*, Vol. I. New York: Harper and Row.

____. 1992. *The Structures of Everyday Life*. Translation from French revised by Siân Reynolds. Civilization and Capitalism, 15th–18th Century, Vol. 1. Berkeley: University of California Press.

Chayanov, A.V. 1966. *A.V. Chayanov on the Theory of Peasant Economy*. Edited by D. Thorner, B. Kerblay, and R.E.F. Smith. Madison: University of Wisconsin Press.

____. 1989. *The Peasant Economy: Collected Works*. Moscow: Ekonomika.

Clapp, J. 2012a. *The Financialization of Food: Who Is Being Fed?* International Studies Association.

____. 2012b. *Food*. Malden, MA: Polity Press.

____. 2014a. "Financialization, Distance and Global Food Politics." *Journal of Peasant Studies* 41, 5.

____. 2014b. "Food Security and Food Sovereignty: Getting Past the Binary." *Dialogues in Human Geography* 4, 2.

____. 2017. *Bigger Is Not Always Better: The Drivers and Implications of the Recent Agribusiness Megamergers*. Waterloo, ON: Global Food Politics Group, University of Waterloo.

Clapp, J., and R. Isakson. 2018a. "Risky Returns: The Implications of Financialization in the Food System." *Development and Change* 49, 2.

____. 2018b. *Speculative Harvests: Financialization, Food, and Agriculture*. Black Point, NS: Fernwood Publishing.

Clapp, J., R. Isakson, and O. Visser. 2016. "The Complex Dynamics of Agriculture as a Financial Asset: Introduction to a Symposium." *Agriculture and Human Values* 34, 1.

Coleman, W., W. Grant, and T. Josling. 2004. *Agriculture in the New Global Economy*. Cheltenham, UK: Edward Elgar.

Coleman, W., and S. Wayland. 2006. "The Origins of Global Civil Society and Nonterritorial Governance: Some Empirical Reflections." *Global Governance* 12, 3 (July–September).

Conti, M. 2012. "Agrofinancialization: Food Price Volatility and Global Value Chains." In *Right to Food and Nutrition Watch*. FIAN International. righttofoodandnutrition.org/files/R_t_F_a_N_Watch_2012_eng.pdf.

Copeland, N. 2019. "Meeting Peasants Where They Are: Cultivating Agroecological Alternatives in Neoliberal Guatemala." *Journal of Peasant Studies* 46, 4.

Council of Economic Advisers. 2008. *Economic Report of the President*. fraser.

stlouisfed.org/files/docs/publications/ERP/2008/ERP_2008.pdf.

CSM. 2011. "Proposals for Next Steps on Food Price Volatility (FPV)." International Food Security and Nutrition Civil Society Mechanism. cso4cfs.files.wordpress.com/2011/06/proposals-for-next-steps-on-food-price-volatility.pdf.

Deering, J. 2017. "Policy Roundtable." *SeedWorld*, May 21, 2017. seedworld.com/policy-roundtable/.

Desmarais, A-A. 2002. "Peasants Speak — The Vía Campesina: Consolidating an International Peasant and Farm Movement." *The Journal of Peasant Studies* 29, 2.

____. 2007. *La Vía Campesina*. Halifax, NS: Fernwood Publishing.

Duncan, J., and M. Zanella. 2016. "The Future of CFS? Critical Directions and Emerging Issues." *Food Governance* (blog), October 31, 2016. foodgovernance.com/the-future-of-cfs-critical-directions-and-emerging-issues/.

The Economist. 2003. "Tequila Sunset in Cancún," September 17. economist.com/unknown/2003/09/17/tequila-sunset-in-cancun.

Edelman, M., and S. Borras Jr. 2016. *The Political Dynamics of Transnational Agrarian Movements.* Halifax, NS: Fernwood Publishing.

Epstein, G. 2005. "Introduction: Financialization and the World Economy." In *Financialization and the World Economy*, edited by G. Epstein. Cheltenham, UK: Edward Elgar Publishing.

____. 2008. "Commodities: Who's Behind the Boom?" *Barron's*, March 31, 2008. barrons.com/articles/SB120674485506173053.

____. 2015. "Financialization: There's Something Happening Here." Political Economy Research Institute Working Paper 394. peri.umass.edu/publication/item/684-financialization-there-s-something-happening-here.

ETC Group. 2015. *Breaking Bad: Big Ag Mega-Mergers in Play: Dow + DuPont in the Pocket? Next: Demonsanto?* ETC Group Communiqué 115. etcgroup.org/sites/www.etcgroup.org/files/files/etc_breakbad_23dec15.pdf.

European Environment Agency. 2015. "Agriculture and Climate Change." eea.europa.eu/signals/signals-2015/articles/agriculture-and-climate-change.

European Seed. 2017. "World Seed Congress Ushers in Era of Openness." May 30. european-seed.com/2017/05/world-seed-congress-ushers-era-openness/.

Evans, P. 2008. "Is an Alternative Globalization Possible?" *Politics & Society* 36, 2.

Fairbairn, M. 2014. "'Like Gold with Yield': Evolving Intersections between Farmland and Finance." *Journal of Peasant Studies* 41, 5.

FAO. n.d.a "Introducing the UN Decade of Family Farming." fao.org/family-farming-decade/home/en/

____. n.d.b "Second International Symposium on Agroecology." fao.org/about/meetings/second-international-agroecology-symposium/about-the-symposium/ar/.

____. 1996. *Report of the World Food Summit.* fao.org/docrep/003/w3548e/w3548e00.htm.

____. 2004. *First World Conference on Organic Seed.* fao.org/3/at732e/at732e.pdf.

____. 2009. *Reform of the Committee on World Food Security.* fao.org/3/k7197e/k7197e.pdf.

____. 2010. *The State of Food Insecurity in the World: Addressing Food Insecurity in Protracted Crises.* fao.org/3/i1683e/i1683e.pdf.

___. 2011. *The State of World Food Insecurity in the World: How Does International Price Volatility Affect Domestic Economies and Food Security?* fao.org/3/i2330e/i2330e.pdf.

___. 2013. *FAO Strategy for Partnerships with Civil Society Organizations.* fao.org/3/a-i3443e.pdf.

___. 2014a. "Legacy of IYFF 2014 and the Way Forward." fao.org/3/b-mm296e.pdf.

___. 2014b. *The State of Food and Agriculture: Innovation in Family Farming.* fao.org/3/i4040e/i4040e.pdf.

___. 2016a. *Proceedings of the FAO International Symposium on the Role of Agricultural Biotechnologies in Sustainable Food Systems and Nutrition. Chapter 8: Final Plenary Session.* fao.org/3/bo984e/bo984e.pdf

___. 2016b. *The State of Food and Agriculture: Climate Change, Agriculture and Food Security.* fao.org/3/i6030e/i6030e.pdf

___. 2017a. *Key Messages for the FAO Regional Meeting on Agricultural Biotechnologies in Sustainable Food Systems and Nutrition in Asia-Pacific.* fao.org/3/I8622EN/i8622en.pdf

___. 2018a. *2nd International Symposium on Agroecology: Scaling Up Agroecology to Achieve the Sustainable Development Goals (SDGs).* fao.org/3/CA0346EN/ca0346en.pdf

___. 2018b. *The 10 Elements of Agroecology: Guiding the Transition to Sustainable Food and Agricultural Systems.* fao.org/3/I9037EN/i9037en.pdf.

___. 2018c. *The International Symposium on Agricultural Innovation for Family Farmers: Unlocking the Potential of Agricultural Innovation to Achieve the Sustainable Development Goals. Chair's Summary.* fao.org/3/CA2632EN/ca2632en.pdf.

___. 2019a. *Report of the 26th Session of the Committee on Agriculture.* fao.org/3/my349en/my349en.pdf.

___. 2019b. "Global Treaty Critical for Saving Disappearing Plants amid Climate Change." fao.org/news/story/en/item/1250594/icode/.

Fasianos, A., G. Diego, and P. Christos. 2016. *Have We Been Here Before? Phases of Financialization within the 20th Century in the United States.* Levy Economics Institute Working Paper 869. levyinstitute.org/pubs/wp_869.pdf.

Ferreira, F.P. 2017. "Financialization and an Era of Crisis on Capitalism." Working paper for presentation at the annual meeting of the American Economic Association, Chicago, January. aeaweb.org/conference/2017/preliminary/paper/t5SZbHiz.

Fligstein, G. 1990. *The Transformation of Corporate Control.* Cambridge: Harvard University Press.

Former Capacity4dev Member. 2022. "The Role of Agricultural Biotechnologies in Sustainable Food Systems and Nutrition — International FAO Symposium 15–17 January 2016," December 8. europa.eu/capacity4dev/hunger-foodsecurity-nutrition/blog/role-agricultural-biotechnologies-sustainable-food-systems-and-nutrition-international-fao-symp.

Foster, J.B. 2007. "The Financialization of Capitalism." *Monthly Review* 58, 11.

___. 2008. "The Financialization of Capital and the Crisis." *Monthly Review* 59, 11.

Foster, J.B., and F. Magdoff. 2014. "Stagnation and Financialization: The Nature of the

Contradiction." *Monthly Review* 66, 1.

Friends of the Earth International. 2015. *Financialization of Nature*. foei.org/wp-content/uploads/2015/11/FoEI-financialization-of-nature-ENG.pdf.

Froud, J., C. Haslam, S. Johal, and K. Williams. 2000. "Shareholder Value and Financialization: Consultancy Promises, Management Moves." *Economy and Society* 29, 1.

Fuglie, K., P. Helsey, J. King, and D. Schimmelpfennig. 2012. "Rising Concentration in Agricultural Input Industries Influences New Farm Technologies." *Amber Waves*, 4.

Fumagalli A., and S. Lucarelli. 2011. "Valorization and Financialization in Cognitive Biocapitalism." *Investment Management and Financial Innovations* 8, 1.

Gaarde, I. 2017. *Peasants Negotiating a Global Policy Space*. London: Routledge.

Ghosh, J. 2005. "Can the US Continue to Rule the World Economy?" In *US Economy: Issues and Perspectives*, edited by N. Janardan Rao. ICFAI Press.

____. 2010. "The Unnatural Coupling: Food and Global Finance." *Journal of Agrarian Change* 10, 1.

____. 2011. "Frenzy in Food Markets." *Truthout*, January 23. truthout.org/articles/frenzy-in-food-markets/.

Harvey, D. 2003. *The New Imperialism*. Oxford: Oxford University Press.

High Level Panel of Experts on Food Security and Nutrition. 2011. *Price Volatility and Food Security*. Rome: Committee on World Food Security.

Hortidaily. 2017. "Copa and Cogeca Underline Need to Develop New and Better Plant Varieties," September 29. hortidaily.com/article/37946/Copa-and-Cogeca-underline-need-to-develop-new-and-better-plant-varieties/.

Hough, A.P. 2019. "The Winding Paths of Peripheral Proletarianization: Local Labour, World Hegemonies, and Crisis in Rural Colombia." *Journal of Agrarian Change* 19, 3.

Howard, P. 2008. "Seed Industry Structure 1996–2008." seedquest.com/statistics/pdf/seedindustrystructure.pdf.

____. 2018. "Seed Industry Structure 1996–2018." philhowardnet.files.wordpress.com/2018/12/Seed2018-1.pdf.

IFAP (International Federation of Agricultural Producers). 1994. *Farmers for a Sustainable Future: The Leadership Role of Agriculture*. Paris.

____. 1995. *Negotiating Linkages: Farmers' Organizations, Agricultural Research and Extension*. web.worldbank.org/archive/website00967A/WEB/PDF/IFAP_DS2.PDF.

International Co-operative Alliance and the United Nations Department for Policy Coordination and Sustainable Development. 1995. *Contribution of Co-operative Enterprises and the International Co-operative Movement to Implementation of UN AGENDA 21: Programme of Action for Sustainable Development*. gdrc.org/icm/uwcc-biblio.html.

IFOAM. 2017. *Compatibility of Breeding Techniques in Organic Systems*. ifoam.bio/sites/default/files/2020-03/Breeding_position_paper_v01_web_0.pdf.

IMAA (Institute for Mergers, Acquisitions and Alliances). 2018. "Number & Value of M&A Worldwide." Accessed October 2018. imaa-institute.org/mergers-and-acquisitions-statistics/.

IMF. 2006. *Global Financial Stability Report: Market Developments and Issues.* Washington, DC: International Monetary Fund (World Economic and Financial Surveys).

___. 2016. *Global Financial Stability Report—Fostering Stability in a Low-Growth, Low-Rate Era.* imf.org/en/Publications/GFSR/Issues/2016/12/31/Fostering-Stability-in-a-Low-Growth-Low-Rate-Era.

International Labour Office. 2012. *Dissolution of the International Federation of Agricultural Producers.* ilo.org/wcmsp5/groups/public/---ed_norm/---relconf/documents/meetingdocument/wcms_183413.pdf.

International Seed Federation. 2016. "Plant Breeding Innovation: Consistent Criteria for the Scope of Regulatory Oversight." seedinnovation.ca/wp-content/uploads/2016/11/4-Ellen-2016_Nov-ISF-PBI-to-CSTA.pdf.

___. 2017a. "How to Talk about Plant Breeding Innovation." corporateeurope.org/sites/default/files/attachments/isf_pbi_discussion-guide_feb-2017.pdf.

___. 2017b. "Milestones in Plant Breeding." worldseed.org/wp-content/uploads/2017/10/MILESTONES_FINAL.pdf.

International Union for the Protection of New Varieties of Plants. 2021. *Guidelines for DNA-Profiling: Molecular Marker Selection and Database Construction ("BMT Guidelines").* upov.int/edocs/infdocs/en/upov_inf_17.pdf.

IPC (International Planning Committee for Food Sovereignty). 2015. "Declaration on Agroecology – Nyéléni." foodsovereignty.org/wp-content/uploads/2015/02/Download-declaration-Agroecology-Nyeleni-2015.pdf.

___. 2020. *Peoples' Food Sovereignty.* foodsovereignty.org/wp-content/uploads/2020/06/IPC_Handbook_EN.pdf.

IPES-Food. 2017. *Too Big to Feed: Exploring the Impacts of Mega-Mergers, Concentration, Concentration of Power in the Agri-Food Sector.* ipes-food.org/_img/upload/files/Concentration_FullReport.pdf.

Isakson, S.R. 2014. "Food and Finance: The Financial Transformation of Agro-Food Supply Chains." *Journal of Peasant Studies* 41, 5.

___. 2015. "Derivatives for Development? Small-Farmer Vulnerability and the Financialization of Climate Risk Management." *Journal of Agrarian Change* 15, 4.

Karl, M. (ed.). 1996. *Partners for Food Security.* fao.org/3/w3055e/w3055e.pdf.

Kastler, G. 2016. "FAO Must Support Peasants' Selection and Condemn the Seizure of Cropped Biodiversity by Patented Genes." In *Proceedings of the FAO International Symposium on the Role of Agricultural Biotechnologies in Sustainable Food Systems and Nutrition*, edited by J. Ruane, J. D. Dargie and C. Daly. Rome: FAO.

Keohane, R., and S. Nye Jr. 2000. "Introduction." In *Governing in a Globalizing World*, edited by S. Nye Jr. and J. Donahue. Brookings Institution Press.

Kotz, D. 2008. *The Financial and Economic Crisis of 2008: A Systemic Crisis of Neoliberal Capitalism.* Amherst: Department of Economics, University of Massachusetts.

___. 2015. "Capitalism and Forms of Capitalism: Levels of Abstraction in Economic Crisis Theory." *Review of Radical Political Economics* 47, 4.

Krippner, G. 2004. *What Is Financialization?* Los Angeles: University of California.

___. 2005. "The Financialization of the American Economy." *Socio-Economic Review* 3, 2.

Krippner, G., B. Lemoine, and Q. Ravelli. 2017. "The Politics of Financialization." *Revue de la régulation* 22. journals.openedition.org/regulation/12637.

Lapavitsas, C. 2011. "Theorizing Financialization." *Work, Employment and Society* 25, 4.

Lenin, V.I. 1964. *The Development of Capitalism in Russia*. Moscow: Progress Publishers.

Margulis, M., and J. Duncan. 2016. "Global Food Security Governance: Key Actors, Issues, and Dynamics." In *Critical Perspectives in Food Studies*, edited by M. Koç, J. Sumner, and A. Winson. Don Mills, ON: Oxford University Press.

Markoff, J. 1996. *Waves of Democracy: Social Movements and Political Change*. Thousand Oaks, CA: Pine Forge Press.

Martin, S.J., and J. Clapp. 2015. "Finance for Agriculture or Agriculture for Finance?" *Journal of Agrarian Change* 15.

Marx, K. 1967. *Capital*, 3 vols. New York: International Publishers.

McKeon, N. 2009. *The United Nations and Civil Society: Legitimating Global Governance—Whose Voice?* New York: Zed Books.

____. 2015. "La Vía Campesina: The 'Peasants' Way' to Changing the System, Not the Climate." *Journal of World-Systems Research* 21, 2.

____ 2016. *Food Security Governance: Empowering Communities, Regulating Corporations*. New York: Routledge.

____. 2017. "Are Equity and Sustainability a Likely Outcome When Foxes and Chickens Share the Same Coop? Critiquing the Concept of Multistakeholder Governance of Food Security." *Globalizations* 14, 3.

McMichael, P. 2005. "Global Development and the Corporate Food Regime." *Research in Rural Sociology and Development* 11.

____. 2009. "Global Citizenship and Multiple Sovereignties: Reconstituting Modernity." In *Hegemonic Transitions, the State and Crisis in Neoliberal Capitalism*, edited by Y. Atasoy. New York: Routledge.

____. 2012. "The Land Grab and Corporate Food Regime Restructuring." *Journal of Peasant Studies* 39, 3/4.

Moore, J.W. 2000. "Environmental Crises and the Metabolic Rift in World-Historical Perspective." *Organization & Environment* 13, 2.

____. 2003. "Capitalism as World-Ecology: Braudel and Marx on Environmental History." *Organization & Environment* 16, 4.

____. 2007. "Ecology and the Rise of Capitalism." PhD dissertation, University of California, Berkeley.

____. 2008. "Ecological Crises and the Agrarian Question in World-Historical Perspective." *Monthly Review* 60, 6.

____. 2010a. "'Amsterdam Is Standing on Norway,' Part I: The Alchemy of Capital." *Journal of Agrarian Change* 10, 1.

____. 2010b. "'Amsterdam Is Standing on Norway,' Part II: The Global North." *Journal of Agrarian Change* 10, 2.

____. 2010c. "The End of the Road? Agricultural Revolutions in the Capitalist World-Ecology, 1450–2010." *Journal of Agrarian Change* 10, 3.

____. 2011. "Transcending the Metabolic Rift." *Journal of Peasant Studies* 38, 1.

____. 2012. "Cheap Food & Bad Money." *Review* 33, 2/3.

Mori, S., and A. Onorati. 2017. *New Breeding Techniques: Which Risks? And Which Regulation Should Be Applied to Them?* Centro Internazionale Crocevia. croceviaterra.it/diritti-dei-contadini-alle-sementi/new-breeding-techniques-which-risks-and-which-regulation-should-be-applied-to-them/.

Morton, A.D. 2007. *Unravelling Gramsci: Hegemony and Passive Revolution in the Global Economy*. London: Pluto Press.

Mulvany, P. 1997. "Beyond the World Food Summit." *Development in Practice* 7, 3.

Newell, J. 2008. "Commodity Speculation's 'Smoking Gun.'" *Probalytics: Probability Analytics Research*, November 17.

NGO/CSO Forum for Food Sovereignty. 2002. "Food Sovereignty: A Right for All." nyeleni.org/en/food-sovereignty-a-right-for-all/.

NGO Forum. 1996. "Profit for Few and Food for All." iatp.org/sites/default/files/Profit_for_Few_or_Food_for_All.htm.

Nyéléni. 2007. "Declaration of Nyéléni." nyeleni.org/IMG/pdf/DeclNyeleni-en.pdf.

OECD. 2018. *Concentration in Seed Markets: Potential Effects and Policy Responses*. Paris: OECD Publishing.

Orhangazi, Ö. 2007. "Financialization and Capital Accumulation in the Non-Financial Corporate Sector: A Theoretical and Empirical Investigation of the U.S. Economy: 1973–2003." Political Economy Research Institute Working Paper 149. scholarworks.umass.edu/cgi/viewcontent.cgi?article=1120&context=peri_workingpapers.

Palley, T.I. 2007. "Financialization: What It Is and Why It Matters." Levy Economics Institute Working Paper 525. levyinstitute.org/pubs/wp_525.pdf.

____. 2013. *Financialization: The Economics of Finance Capital Domination*. London: Palgrave Macmillan.

Perez, I. 2013. "Climate Change and Rising Food Prices Heightened Arab Spring." *Scientific American*, March 4, 2013. scientificamerican.com/article/climate-change-and-rising-food-prices-heightened-arab-spring/.

Peschard K., and S. Randeria. 2019. "JPS Special Forum on Seed Activism: An Overview of the Issues." *Journal of Peasant Studies*. https://doi.org/10.1080/03066150.2019.1578752.

Phillips, K. 1993. *Boiling Point: Republicans, Democrats, and the Decline of Middle-Class Prosperity*. New York: Random House.

Russi, L. 2014. *In pasto al capitale. Le mani della finanza sul cibo*. Rome: Castelvecchi.

Sassen, S. 2001. *The Global City: New York, London, Tokyo*. Princeton, NJ: Princeton University Press.

Scott, J.C., and B. Kerkvliet (eds.). 1986. *Everyday Forms of Peasant Resistance in Southeast Asia*. London: Frank Cass.

Sivini, G. 2009. "Scommesse sulla fame: Finanza, agribusiness e crisi alimentare." *Foedus* 24.

Smith, N. 2007. "Nature as Accumulation Strategy." *Socialist Register*, 43.

Subsidiary Body for Scientific and Technological Advice. 2016. *Workshop on the Identification of Adaptation Measures, Taking into Account the Diversity of the Agricultural Systems, Indigenous Knowledge Systems and the Differences in Scale as well as Possible Co-Benefits and Sharing Experiences in Research and Development and On-The-Ground Activities, Including Socioeconomic, Environmental and*

Gender Aspects. United Nations Framework Convention on Climate Change. businessdocbox.com/Agriculture/67140039-Fccc-sbsta-2016-inf-5.html.

Sweezy, P.M. 1997. "More (or Less) on Globalization." *Monthly Review* 49, 4.

Tarrow, S. 2005. *The New Transnational Activism.* New York: Cambridge University Press.

Tilly, C. 1995. *Popular Contention in Great Britain: 1758–1834.* Cambridge, MA: Harvard University Press.

Union of Concerned Scientists. 2009. *Failure to Yield: Biotechnology's Broken Promises.* grist.org/wp-content/uploads/2010/09/failure-to-yield-brochure.pdf.

United Nations. 1992a. "Agenda 21. Chapter 14: Promoting Sustainable Agriculture and Rural Development." un-documents.net/a21-14.htm.

____. 1992b. *Status and Role of Cooperatives in the Light of New Economic and Social Trends: Report of the Secretary-General.* digitallibrary.un.org/record/144848.

____. 2002. *Plan of Implementation of the World Summit on Sustainable Development.* un.org/esa/sustdev/documents/WSSD_POI_PD/English/WSSD_PlanImpl.pdf.

____. 2018. *United Nations Declaration on the Rights of Peasants and Other People Working in Rural Areas.* digitallibrary.un.org/record/1650694/files/A_HRC_RES_39_12-EN.pdf.

United Nations Framework Convention on Climate Change. 2016. *The Paris Agreement.* unfccc.int/sites/default/files/resource/parisagreement_publication.pdf.

U.S. Bureau of Economic Analysis. 2013. *National Income and Product Table 1.14,* February 28. bea.gov.

van der Ploeg, J.D. 2010. "The Peasantries of the Twenty-First Century: The Commoditisation Debate Revisited." *Journal of Peasant Studies* 37, 1.

Vander Stichele, M. 2014. "How Financialisation Influences the Dynamics in the Food Supply Chain." Stichting Onderzoek Multinationale Ondernemingen. farmlandgrab.org/uploads/attachment/Discussion_Paper_-_Myriam_Vander_Stichele_-_final_for_print.pdf.

Vía Campesina. 1999. "Seattle Declaration: Take WTO out of Agriculture." viacampesina.org/en/seattle-declaration-take-wto-out-of-agriculture/.

____. 2003. "Food Sovereignty." viacampesina.org/en/food-sovereignty/.

____. 2006. "United in the Vía Campesina." viacampesina.org/en/united-in-the-vcampesina/.

____. 2014. "International Symposium on Agroecology at the FAO in Rome." viacampesina.org/en/international-symposium-on-agroecology-at-the-fao-in-rome/.

____. 2015. "FAO Symposium on Biotechnology: The Biotechnology Industry Runs the Show." viacampesina.org/en/fao-symposium-on-biotechnology-the-biotechnology-industry-runs-the-show/.

____. 2018. "The Biotech Industry Is Trying to Block the UN Conference on Biodiversity, But It Won't Block Farmers." viacampesina.org/en/the-biotech-industry-is-trying-to-block-the-un-conference-on-biodiversity-but-it-wont-block-farmers/.

Visser, O., N. Mamonova, N. Spoor, and A. Nikulin. 2015. "'Quiet Food Sovereignty'

as Food Sovereignty without a Movement? Insights from Post-Socialist Russia."
Globalizations 12, 4.

Webb, W.P. 1964. *The Great Frontier*. University of Texas Press.

White, S. 2017. "De Castro MEP: New Plant Breeding Techniques Are Nothing Like
'Frankenstein' GMOs." *EUROACTIV*, October 16. euractiv.com/section/agriculture-
food/news/mep-new-plant-breeding-techniques-are-nothing-like-frankenstein-
gmos.

Wolf, P. 1973. *Wars of the Twentieth Century*. London: Faber and Faber.

World Bank. 2008. *World Development Report 2008: Agriculture for Development*.
openknowledge.worldbank.org/bitstream/handle/10986/5990/WDR%20
2008%20-%20English.pdf?sequence=3&isAllowed=y.

World Rainforest Movement. 2012. "Growing Speculation: From the Appropriation
and Commodification to the Financialization of Nature." WRM Bulletin 181.
wrm.org.uy/bulletin-articles/growing-speculation-from-the-appropriation-and-
commodification-to-the-financialization-of-nature.

Zhang, J. 2017. "Summary and Analysis of Mergers between Global Seed Companies
in 2016." *Agronews*, March 1.

Zurayk, R. 2011. *Food, Farming, and Freedom: Sowing the Arab Spring*. Charlottesville,
VA: Just World Books.

Appendix: Establishment of Transnational Agrarian Movements

MAELA (Movimiento Agroecológico Latinoamericano y del Caribe, established 1989) emerged from the crisis caused by the economic policies of the 1980s. It was formally constituted in 1992. It comprises 210 organizations in twenty countries in Mesoamerica–the Caribbean, the Andean region, and Conosur (the Southern Cone of South America), ultimately representing more than one million peasants, Indigenous and small family producers, who work with agroecology. MAELA is a social, pluralistic, democratic, multicultural movement with a focus on agri-food production and rural development, based on the principles of food sovereignty and respect of nature. (maela-agroecologia.org).

Vía Campesina (established 1993) convenes 182 local and national organizations across eighty-one countries, representing more than 200 million farmers and their demands for social justice. It brings together peasants, landless workers, Indigenous people, pastoralists, fishers, migrant farmworkers, small and medium-size farmers, rural women, and peasant youth from across the world. Vía Campesina put forward the concept of food sovereignty. (viacampesina.org)

COPROFAM (Coordinator of Organizations of Family Farmers of Mercosur, established 1994) is an organization integrated by representatives of family producers of the expanded South American trade bloc Mercosur. It is composed of nine organizations from seven countries in South America, representing more than four million rural workers, family farmers, peasants, and Indigenous people. (coprofam.org)

The **World Forum of Fish Harvesters and Fish Workers** (established 1995) formed as a result of a meeting between national organizations for coastal fishing and the fishing industry in Quebec City. It followed the WTO's Doha mandate, which declared the priority of ongoing negotiations was to lift people out of poverty and promote sustainable development. Current WTO negotiations fail to address the concerns of fish harvesters and workers, as well as those of traditional fishing communities worldwide.

The World Forum of Fish Harvesters and Fish Workers aims to uphold fundamental human rights, social justice, and the culture of fish harvesters and fish workers, affirming the sea as the source of all life and committing to sustain fisheries and aquatic resources in order to protect livelihood. (worldfisher-forum.org).

The **World Forum of Fisher Peoples** (established 1997) is a mass-based social movement of small-scale fisher peoples from across the world. It was founded in India by a number of mass-based organizations from the Global South in response to increasing pressure on small-scale fisheries, including habitat destruction, anthropogenic pollution, and the encroachment on small-scale fishing territories by large-scale fishing fleets, illegal fishing, and overfishing. It has twenty-nine member organizations from twenty-three countries and represents over ten million fisher people from across the world. (www.worldfishers.org)

ROPPA (Network of Farmers Organizations and Agricultural Producers of West Africa, established 2000) aims to promote the development of family farms and peasant agriculture while addressing national economic liberalization and globalization of trade policies. It defends the values of a sustainable and efficient peasant agriculture at the service of family farms and agricultural producers. It convenes thirteen national farmer organizations covering countries in West Africa. (roppa-afrique.org)

The **Asia Farmers' Association for Sustainable Rural Development** (established 2002) is an alliance of national farmer organizations composed of small-scale family farmers, fishers, Indigenous Peoples, forest users, herders, and pastoralists. It was established in 2002 after a series of farmers' exchange visits organized by AsiaDHRRA, a regional NGO. Its objective is to "build solidarity, raise a collective voice, and empower members as key drivers and actors for sustainable rural development." (asianfarmers.org)

The **World Alliance of Mobile Indigenous Peoples** (established 2003) is a global network of nomadic peoples practising various forms of mobility as a livelihood strategy based on the sustainable use of natural resources. It aims to establish a common vision among mobile peoples worldwide and promote policies supporting freedom of movement in order to maintain their livelihoods. (wamipglobal.com)

Propac (Plateforme Régionale des Organisations Paysannes d'Afrique

Central, established 2005) brings together ten national farmers' organizations in Central Africa. It aims to influence agricultural policies and improve the livelihoods of rural populations by strengthening their organizations and their advocacy and lobby skills. (infopropac.org).

URGENCI (Urban-Rural networks: GEnerating New forms of exchanges between CItizens, established 2008) is the leading organization for networking and promotion of community-supported agriculture worldwide. (urgenci.net)

Index